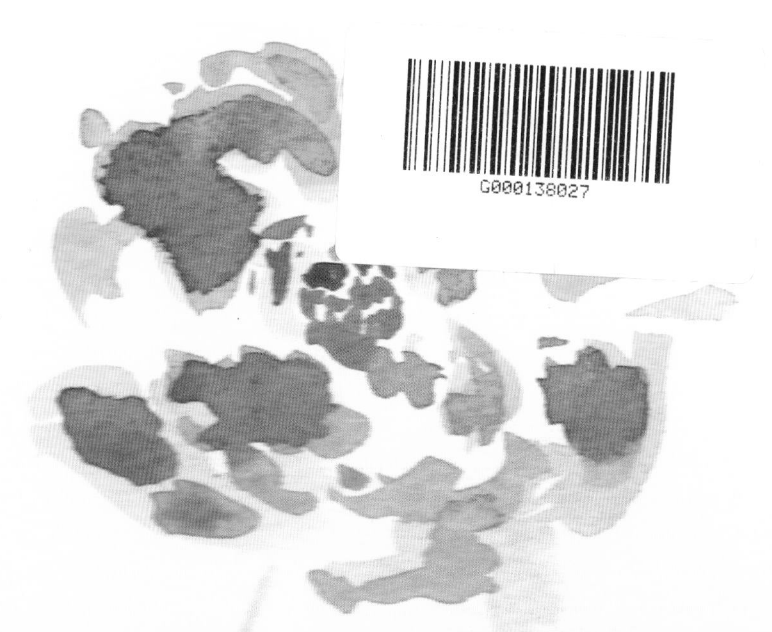

THE LOVE OF A BROTHER

From Plaistow to Passchendaele

THE MEMOIRS OF PRIVATE. F. E. CEARNS

By Percy Cearns

Published in 2011 by Martin Cearns

For all correspondence and general enquiries relating to this book,
please email:
cearnsbooks@postmaster.co.uk

Acknowledgements by Martin Cearns.
My gratitude to the many people with whom I have spoken during 2010
and who gave me help, advice and encouragement to get
this project completed.

Artwork by Edward Cearns.

Printed by
Lynhurst Press, 4 & 5 Yardley Business Park, Luckyn Lane,
Basildon, Essex, SS14 3GL.

Introduction

FRED CEARNS
The Love of a Brother
From Plaistow to Passchendaele

FOR many years there was a private book on my family's shelves. I did not know of its existence until some five years ago when I was turning out my parents' house. I discovered a most fascinating and enlightening read.

The book contained the story of my great uncle, Fred Cearns. It was written by his brother Percy within weeks of Fred's death at the age of 28 in August 1917 at Ypres whilst serving with the London Regiment (Royal Fusiliers). The brothers were clearly very close.

Fred was one of over one million British and Commonwealth soldiers who died in The First World War; but this is a very personal and revealing story. The book has been reproduced as close to the original as possible, including some grammatical inaccuracies that Percy made and idiosyncrasies of his style of writing.

The family home was in Plaistow and Fred and Percy were two of 13 children. The book describes in detail family life in London's East End at the end of the 19th century and as such is an interesting piece of social history. Then as a young man it tells of his playing football including a few games for West Ham United's reserve team at the Boleyn Ground, Upton Park. Their father J W Y(Jimmy) Cearns worked for the Thames Ironworks and was on the first committee when a works team was formed in 1895. He was then one of the inaugural directors when the team went professional and became West Ham United in 1900.

And two of Fred's brothers mentioned in the book also were to play a part in the history of West Ham United. Frank became Secretary from 1946 to 1956 and Will (WJC) was a director from 1924 and Chairman from 1934 until his death in 1950.

In November 1914 Fred responded to the call and enlisted with the army. In the summer of 1915 he was in Gallipoli; and by the summer of 1916 he was on the Somme. In March 1917 he suffered injury and had to return to Blighty for convalescence but he was back and ready for action by the time of the big push near Ypres in July 1917, the campaign which is now known as Passchendaele.

The book tells us much about Fred at this time as Percy was an army dispatch rider and on his days off he was able to use his Triumph motorbike to get to meet up with his brother. History is full of stories of the horrendous conditions in the mud of Flanders and the 1917 battles for Passchendaele, but here we have much interesting and intimate detail of what could happen away from the front line.

Martin Cearns
Loughton, Essex, 2011

THE CERTIFICATE FROM THE COMMONWEALTH WAR GRAVES COMMISSION

In Memory of
Private FREDERICK ERNEST CEARNS

281228, 4th Bn. attd. 3rd Bn., London Regiment (Royal Fusiliers)
who died age 28
on 13 August 1917
Son of Mr. J. W. Y. and Mrs. E. A. Cearns, of 8, Plaistow Park Rd., Plaistow, London.
Enlisted Nov., 1914. Also served at Gallipoli. Previously wounded in March,1917.
Remembered with honour
YPRES (MENIN GATE) MEMORIAL

Commemorated in perpetuity by
the Commonwealth War Graves Commission

The memorial bears the names of 54,000 men from United Kingdom and Commonwealth Forces who fell in the Ypres Salient before 16th August 1917 and who have no known grave. Fred's name can be found on panel 52.

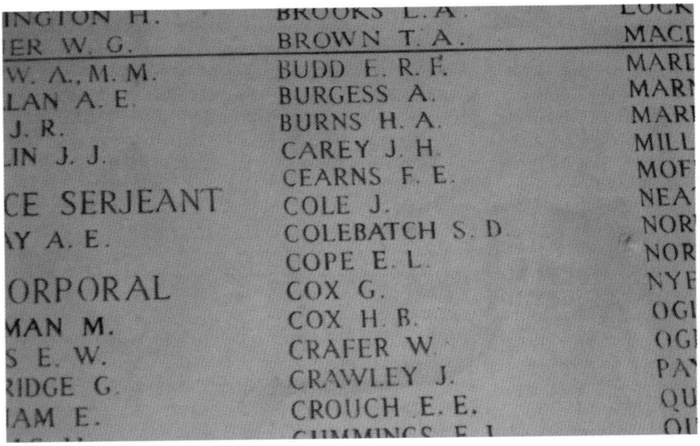

The memoirs of Private F. E. Cearns killed in action

August 15th. 1917.

-:-:-:-:-:-:-:-:-:-:-:-:-:-:-

Dedicated to my dear mother and father.

o
-:-:-:-:-:-:-oOo-:-:-:-:-:-:-
o

Percy Leonard Cearns

PREFACE

IT has been written: "The evil that men do lives after them the good is oft interred with their bones". For my part this sentiment has always seemed cynical and almost untrue. Certainly I cannot believe that such evil as my brother Fred, being human, may have done will be remembered; whereas I am positive his goodness will always be recalled and his memory treasured for his sweet disposition.

In the following memoirs, try as I would, I believe I have failed to convey more than an indication of the wonderful character and true Christian spirit of Frederick Ernest Cearns, who died a private soldier, that we, his countrymen might continue to enjoy the freedom which has always been our inheritance. Nevertheless succeed or fail, I felt it was due to him that somebody should endeavour to write of his simple goodly life and noble death, if only that from such writing may be learned the lessons of how to live and die as a man and a Christian.

For his life was a pattern nobody need fear to copy and a pattern which so many would unfortunately fail to copy correctly.

Therefore, in the long hours following that day when the awful news reached me, and when off duty my thoughts were of him, the idea to write these memoirs came to me. So I have set down just what I have been able to remember of his life as a civilian, during those precious years of peace, and his career and death of a soldier, in the greatest, and it is to be hoped, the last of all wars.

I wish not to speak of his love for me because honestly I think there were very few people for whom he had other sentiments than love. But for my part there is no fellow for whom I can have the admiration almost amounting to veneration, which I felt and feel for my brother Fred. And this feeling is shared by many of those, both relatives and friends who knew him. What better testimony than this is necessary to prove his worth? Privileged to live many long years of happiness with him, privileged to be with him so near the end and now privileged to write of him, in all reverence I say that many of us may pray that when our time comes, we may be as worthy as he to meet the creator.

And to my dear mother and father, for whom these pages are chiefly written, may I write a wish that they will find some consolation and fleeting moments of even happiness as they read the following lines.

The measure for their love for him was the love he had for them, dearly as son ever loved parents.

Percy Leonard Cearns
September, 1917

PART ONE

CIVILIAN

FREDERICK ERNEST CEARNS, a hero, a gentleman, and a Christian. Above and before all, a Christian.

Private F. E. Cearns, No. 281228, just a cipher amongst the teeming millions known collectively as the British Army; No. 281228 – and that is all that concerns the general public; just another in the long list of killed, published all too often in the daily papers. One more sacrificed to the power lust of Germany; but what a willing sacrifice. Yes, that was the key note of all his actions in the Army, for his country; always willing to do all and give all, never detracting in the giving, by the slightest symptom of what is recognised as a Tommy's privilege – grumbling. And as during his Military career, so in his civil life it was sacrifice of self, and perfect unselfishness governed every action; so that all who knew him as he lived, know what a true Christian passed to rest in the person of that soldier No. 281228, who, in spite of cannon's roar, went to sleep in that water-logged trench of bloody Flanders, and woke to "peace, perfect peace".

Not a long life had he, just 28 years, but for the good he did in such a short space, we can think God rewarded him by taking him quietly and painlessly. A consoling thought is that.

Fred was born in Canning Town, East London. His birthplace quite an ordinary grocer's shop in an ordinary street – to wit – Swancombe Street; but that grocer's shop, of which I personally recollect very little, was the cradle of our family, and therefore I know must have been a veritable hive of industry. Many anecdotes have I from Dad, which confirms this impression; sometimes I must confess that these anecdotes lead me to believe the neighbourhood could hardly be termed aristocratic or even salubrious. But what mattered that to the Cearns happy family, it was here my brother first saw light of day on the 29th January 1889. He was the 10th child and was a bit of a "tarter", if I remember rightly what I have heard. Of just the right age to nurse him were his two sisters Edie and Annie, now Fred had an aversion for the former and an affection for the latter, whilst I, who appeared on life's stage 21 months later than he, loved Edie.

Nature's law of compensation here is well illustrated. What could have been better? Annie became Fred's nurse while Edie was troubled with the care of my person. I wonder did we then learn to form fours and to do other manoeuvres for fighting; for of course we must have had our battles. If after life is any criterion, I am afraid that I was seldom victorious. Even then, I guess, Fred could "out-stick" me, and I warrant would out-do his poor nurse. Edie must have had an easy job, for I was always a "lazy dog", but I pity poor Annie. Well, as I have said, I was too young to take a lively interest in details of life at that shop, but I suppose Fred was baptised, vaccinated, had teeth, grew hair, learned to walk, then to talk, and finally had measles; the last much to his sisters' delight, who, as a consequence had a long vacation from school. There was also a grandmother who, I believe used to act as our guardian when Ma appeared with an admonitory cane. I do not know that the public house next door interested Fred more than I, except to watch huge barrels roll off carts, and disappear into the yawning and insatiable depths beneath that popular resort. Many a time since then have Fred and I sat for hours listening to Dad discoursing on the customers that flowed from our neighbour's shop to ours – after closing time. How many tussles he had I do not know, for Dad was not always 60 and "rheumaticky". How I have seen Fred laugh at some of mother's shop yarns too. One of these is of a youth who crept in and slowly enticed a "German" sausage off the counter. Ma spotted it as it made its exit in the youth's hand at top speed out of the door. A friendly baker – one of the "Kaiser Bill's" people – Schmidt, who lived opposite, was called on to chase that disappearing youth and sausage. The result of the chase I have forgotten, but I have often wondered since if Schmidt was a spy. By the way, I have forgotten to give Mother's battle cry as she waved him on; t'was this: "There goes my German sausage".

Such tales as this have often made Fred and we others laugh long and loud round the home fireside.

Exactly why, when, and how it was, I do not know.

But Fred was about six-years-old, (a dear, pale, fair headed little boy, Ma called him) when the family shifted its headquarters to sweet, suburban,

Selwyn Road. Memories of a good garden, and nasty next door neighbours are all I have of this place. Whether it was these neighbours or the fact of outgrowing the house, I do not know, but after about six months in this place, the family again transferred itself, to that home of homes, 8 Plaistow Park Road. Here it has been ever since, which is to say about 21 years. How it has dwindled though; then, we were 11 children and Mother and Dad, now at home there are just the two last arrivals, Grace and Nelly, and that same dear old Ma and Dad.

I think my mind must have been far from retentive at this period for I recollect little of the incidents of Fred's life for several years. However, shortly after this last move I was "down and out" with diphtheria, contracted in trying to make some friends with a gutter drain. Though I cannot remember, I guess, during any illness Fred was very concerned about me; he always was.

My mind next recalls our first school days together at Credon Road School. We used to wander through those alley-ways, to and from school in company. A tale of a wicked old witch there was, who had her cave in one of those alleys. How we used to run by there in the dusk of the winter evenings. Fred was a class above me, so as regards his brain powers I have no details, for we were not together. I can vouch for his sporting proclivities however, for here it was he first showed his liking for kicking a two penny rubber ball about, in the playground.

The year 1898 saw our studies transferred to Balaam St School. Fred was in standard 3 whilst I was in standard 2. For six happy years we were together here. At his lessons they saw Fred was not brilliant but very thorough, and a plodder. Such a thing as leaving a job undone he would not think of. All the time at this school he was never absent, never late, and gained prizes for good conduct and regular attendance, much to my secret jealousy. At the prize distributions, however, how proud I felt that his name was called out amongst other lucky ones, he would march out in front of the 400 boys and receive his book or medal. And what a favourite he was with everybody, teachers and boys alike, they really loved him I think, for he had such an unusually even temper and good disposition. If he had a fault it was obstinacy, this, however, stood him in good stead in many ways, for his was the obstinacy which never recognised defeat in anything. When recently on leave all the teachers who I saw at this school eagerly asked for details regarding Fred. They seemed proud to have had such a fellow to teach. Read the letter of sympathy sent by our dear old headmaster, Mr David Fist. Here are two extracts: "He was a lad of the best sort for whose character I had great admiration; just the kind that we can least spare. He laid down his life willingly for a cause that we cannot allow to fail, for it was the cause of humanity". Ask his teachers of their opinion of him as a boy. Their unanimous reply would be on the lines indicated in the above.

On the football field what a hero he used to appear to youngsters. He was captain of the school team for two years, I think. In addition he was frequently chosen to play for the picked boy team for the West Ham schools, against teams from other districts. This, we boys always consider a great honour, and undoubtedly it was, and indicated to some extent Fred's powers at the game. But even as a boy he would never boast of anything that he could do and seemed quite unconcerned whenever he was chosen for this game. As centre forward or outside-right, what havoc he used to make among the opposing defences. In after years I have played against him so I know what they must have endured. I have seen him, when the school was losing a match, clench his teeth, and with the ball at this toe race through the opponents time after time, scoring goals until the game was won. Knocks he would give and take, but always in the best of spirit. He would never trip a fellow up at football; if an opponent were on the ground he would sooner stop and help him up than run by him. In after life he was the same, never "hitting a fellow when he was down" but "always helping lame dogs over stiles".

As a youngster I was a bit of a "lame dog" physically. How he used to pity me. Many a time when the cold winter winds have made me gasp for breath, has he sheltered me with his coat as he helped me along to school. "Thoughtless as a schoolboy" is an expression sometimes used. If all schoolboys were like Fred this should be "thoughtful as a schoolboy". He would not have hurt a fly. During his last year at school, we were in classes together, he in standard 7 and I in standard 6. What a paternal eye he kept on me. "Young Percy" he would call me. I guess every time I was punished, which was quite frequent, it hurt him more than if it were his hands that were being tickled with the cane. At home during these years, I suppose we had boyish quarrels. The most serious of these, however, would be as to whose turn it was to fetch the coals. You see I always wanted to arrange it so that he did all the coals carrying, even his temper would not submit to this.

We used to be the best of friends while playing in the street. What terrors of Plaistow Park Road we lads must have been. I wonder how many fruitless journeys to open front doors we have caused ladies in the neighbourhood through our propensity to play a game, colloquially known as "knocking down ginger". "Kick can", "buttons", "egg cap", "leap frog", "robbers and thieves" were among other famous sports which we young ruffians were wont to pass our evenings. Dad never believed in restraining us from roaming the streets. I think he was right too. I wonder where our comrades of those days are now. Probably some died as my brother has, whilst others are even now scattered over the different battlefields fighting for the "cause". Wherever they are however, I guess none of them will have forgotten Fred Cearns, and all will have only good to say of him. Just a few years ago, Jimmy Wilson, a great friend of his, who has prospered, came to see him. How fond he was of Fred could easily be seen. Poor Duncan MacDonald was another chum of his. He, poor lad, died when about 15-years-old.

One of the most popular playing grounds as we got into our teens was Phillip's work yard. What days we used to spend there. Arthur and Stanley Cook, Tommy Mumford, Harry and Fred Franks, and Fred and I.

"Kick can" was our regular pastime; and what a pastime; unless we spoiled one suit of clothes a fortnight by rents and dirt, we were none of us content. There we used to climb into or under dirty old carts, on to much-laden shelves, behind sooty forges, down into smelly pits. Even the pungent paint shop did not escape us and many a trace of this haunt did our clothes show. Mr Scales and "Old Steve", what a time we used to give them. As a variation to this we would try football or even cricket, but huge carts and piles of wheels on the field did not make for enjoyment when playing these games; so we would often abandon such sports for "swinging the sledge hammer". I don't know who was the best at this, but I bet it was Fred. Personally, I used to swing that dreadful implement until my muscles felt fit to burst and I looked to be on the verge of apoplexy, and then somebody else would just about double the number of my swings. Sometimes we would be asked to tea by Mrs Phillips, much to our secret satisfaction. Then we would outstay our welcome playing darts with Arthur and Stanley.

From these evenings we would return home quite clean, much to Mother's astonishment. Frank was rather interested in these visits of ours, for he knew there were certain Misses Cook. I can well remember how he used to question us about these girls – particularly Altro. I think the name and the curls attracted him then. Anyhow, as we know, the sequel has been most romantic. One incident of this playground of ours I have omitted to mention. To flatter ourselves we were helping the work, we would roll huge iron cart wheels' tyres from one yard to another, some 200 yards distant. This meant traversing a rather busy road. These tyres had just come from the forges and were still very hot at one invisible spot. Arthur and Stan Cook were quite adept through long practice at assisting even two hoops, each twice as big as themselves, along the road, without ever handling the warm spot. Poor Fred one day, wishing to emulate them to some extent, volunteered to wheel a huge tyre across to the outer shop. Away he went quite steadily at first. Presently a wobble began. This was accentuated to some extent when Fred, in steering it, grabbed hold of the hot place.

Across the road the thing flew and was only stopped by the kerb and an old bad tempered lady who happened to be on the spot. I believe she burnt her hand among other injuries. What ensued I do not exactly know, but as a result we visitors to the yard used to have to content ourselves with watching those clever brothers at the game. I believe Fred was very sorry for the old lady but I do not think he stopped to apologise.

Fred and I shared the same room ever since I can remember. Here as we lay at nights in our beds, we used to exchange our little confidences. Even until he left home for the battlefield was this the case. In our boyhood, these little talks we had, were invariably preceded by some game which can best be accomplished and enjoyed in a bedroom. Generally the bed linen suffered as a result of such frolics. Yes, I must confess we had many a pillow fight in which victory varied. This particular type of pastime was ended by a catastrophe that gave us a chilly bedroom for a few nights, and depleted money boxes for some weeks. It occurred one evening, when after a long and prolonged bout, Fred dealt a wonderful *"coup de grace"* full in the face. Back went my head out into the night by way of a closed window. The glass tinkled on the ground below while we hurriedly scampered to bed and put the light out. Of course we should have received severe chastisement but as usual escaped with a few words of scolding from Ma. However, we decided to alter our games, and as football was becoming very popular with us, we decided to use our bedroom as a practice field for learning to "head" a ball correctly. The ball was made of paper, the goals were the two sides of the bed, while the field of play was the bed itself. Huge fun we had from this very simple, if destructive game. I believe, however, it robbed poor Ma and Dad of many hours sleep, for their room was directly beneath ours, and we were hardly light-footed. Often have we been in the midst of our games, and suddenly looked up to see the stern apparition of Dad standing at our door. At any rate he tried his best to be stern, but he never punished us. In fact, I believe he often wanted to laugh at our nocturnal pranks.

There was a sad period when we could not have these games however. That was when grandmother had her fatal illness. Then Fred said we must not make any noise and we used to creep on tiptoes upstairs and go straight to bed. It was during this time that we took to reading pernicious literature. Our favourite books were the "Boy's Friend", "Boy's Realm", "Union Jack". Night after night we used to "burn midnight oil", devouring the wonderful tales these books contained. How we did enjoy reading of the daring deeds visibly portrayed in these pages – I wonder now whether any heroes either of these or other fictions ever suffered and braved what dear Fred and thousands of others have done during this awful war – naturally this class of reading was "forbidden fruit" to us. Therefore, during the day, we were forced to hide the books beneath articles of furniture in the bedroom and many times we have returned from school to find that Mother had discovered these. Then we received lectures from Dad who always told us there were plenty of books in the bookcase to read "instead of such trash". I am afraid we neither of us took much notice of this advice however, as we would always replace the lost copies and impatiently await the next numbers.

During the winter evenings, when it was dark, what a job it was to get us to go to bed. This was on account of the solemn quietness of that last flight of stairs and the empty bedroom. How we used to manoeuvre to get the other to be first to venture. It was so amusing.

Frank was another inmate of our cosy bedroom. He however was always a late bird, never getting to bed much before midnight, even then he would lay reading far into the small hours, by the extravagant light of two or more candles. One night Fred conceived an idea to cure him of this habit, and at the same time have a joke. The idea did not succeed in the former object, but certainly it was a fine joke. The pieces of various candles which would be used as "reading lamps" pieces of stout thread were tied, the other ends being led under Frank's bed, held by Fred. Great care was taken to hide the thread from the notice of our elder brother, the reader. Then we youngsters extinguished the light and got into our respective beds.

Patiently we waited the arrival of our victim. Presently his steps were heard on the stairs and tight closed were our eyes in well-feigned sleep. Unsuspiciously Frank lit the candles, undressed and slipped between the sheets, then opened his book – I believe it was some such hair-raiser as "Old St Pauls" – and settled down to an enjoyable read. A few minutes lapsed and the candles on their several pieces of thread moved an inch or so. Lying next to Frank I felt him jump, and heard him mutter "what's that". Presently another movement of the sources of illumination, and another start and exclamation by the victim. Finally a big heave by Fred at the threads and on the floor jumped the candles and candlesticks, which luckily were not of chinaware. With one huge jump Frank sat up in bed. I could feel how startled he was. Fred and I with our heads beneath the blankets tried hard to stifle our laughter; but it was impossible, especially when Frank re-lit the candles and discovered the cause of the moving lights. We had to give way to our feelings and have a good laugh. For his part Frank took the joke very well and laughed himself, while calling us "young bounders".

Perhaps he was glad to discover there was no occult explanation of why the candles should jump from the table to the floor. For everybody did laugh when we told them of the joke the next day.

Like good little boys we used to go to church regularly. Had we been asked why this was though, I guess we should have had to reply "because we have to". It might have been because of the nice white surplice that he knew he would wear, or because of the one shilling per month stipend that accrued or again because he really liked singing, at any rate, Fred was soon to be found a member of the church choir. What an innocent little boy he did look, I can well remember. Truth compels me to state, however, that his choirboy life was of short duration. It all came about like this. There were three or four of those good little choirboys in a schoolroom one evening. One of them persisted in ringing a bell loud and long. Enters a stern and masterly clergyman who has been addressing a meeting in the next room.

Questions as to the identity of the author of the ringing without satisfactory results from his point of view, for these lads were "sports".

Result, one month's suspension from the choir for them all. After that Fred never returned to the church as a choirboy. Thus finished that incident in his career.

He must have had a fairly good voice, but in the choir he never sang any solos, neither for that matter could he be prevailed upon to sing a solo at home. Now I was quite the reverse to this. On every possible occasion I would make my voice heard in an endeavour to sing, with a resultant noise that only those who have heard can appreciate. Now every Sunday evening, Ruth or Louie would sit at the piano and play over many fine old hymn tunes. That was a good opportunity for me to exercise my vocal powers. For many Sundays I think Fred must have suffered the noise I made in agonised silence. Finally he could stand it no longer and one Sunday after a more than usually fierce effort on my part, he broke out with words to the effect that I was making a horrible noise – which was true. Of course I howled and he was sent to bed. No sooner than he had uttered the words he would rather have bitten his tongue off than have said them. How sorry he was I can remember to this day. For weeks afterwards he did his best to compensate me for those few hasty words.

It was about this time we were confirmed together. At the time we used to talk about it and what it meant, but I am not quite sure we really understood. When far from home in those last few years, I imagine however, that his mind has often gone back to those occasions when Ma and Dad and almost all the family used to go to early communion together in the years now seemingly long ago.

By this time Fred had of course left school. His first essay at a business career was with a certain firm known as Stubbs & Co., of Fenchurch Street. Possibly he had his foot on the very first rung of the business ladder and was merely an office boy. We however, liked to dignify his position by terming him a junior clerk. As usual he was a favourite, and would probably have succeeded well with these good people but after about 18 months service with them, Dad found better scope for him elsewhere. While at "business in the city" to use a favourite expression, a rather humorous incident occurred. Fred was beginning to look rather ill

Mother's loving eye soon noticed this and possibly thinking that his food was not agreeing with him, she one day asked what he had for dinner. Of course money was given him for the purpose of procuring food, and therefore Mother's surprise can be imagined when his answer was "nothing Mother". Further questioning him elicited the fact that instead of having dinner, the dear youngster would have a "manly" cigarette and a stroll across London Bridge. I guess he had some secret and useful purpose for which he required the extra pocket money. His innate honesty, however, would not permit him even attempting to deceive his mother. She, while calling him a "naughty boy", really wanted to smile I believe. Anyway, the sequel was that he turned all his illicit gains out of his pockets and handed them to Mother. Never again did Fred attempt to content himself with such a meagre dinner as a cigarette must necessarily be. I wonder if his youthful practice of fasting was recalled to his mind when food was scarce during his army life. If so, it is easy to realise how that whimsical smile of his would cross his face at the thought of those dear old days.

Fred's next and last place of business was at Victoria Docks with a firm of ship's chandlers known as Wiggins & Rhill. For 10 years, until he joined the forces, he was with these people and gained for himself the affection and respect of everybody, masters and men alike. The following is an extract from a letter of condolence received from his employers, and indicate a little of what they thought of him.

"We deeply grieved to hear the sad news about poor Fred. We held him in very high esteem, as we always found him a young man of high character and of such a genial disposition that everybody in the firm loved and admired him".

Of his life here Fred would tell so many anecdotes both amusing and serious. Among the latter there was an incident of a fellow worker of his who one day did certain irregular things in connection with the work. Just what these things were, I cannot now remember. A Mr Saunders, one of the firm, – was so annoyed at what had occurred that he offered quite a large sum to the person who would divulge the culprit's name. As it happens Fred was the only one who knew besides the man himself, and he would have been perhaps justified in disclosing his knowledge. As a matter of fact I called him stupid for not doing so for of course he kept the secret. "I cannot do it as he will get dismissed" was his answer. As this dismissal would have meant a rise in position for Fred, one can appreciate even more the value of his good natured reticence. Quite in keeping, however, with his whole character in this incident.

Many amusing yarns has he related to us regarding certain after dinner games of cards at the office, in which even the "young bosses" did not deem it undignified to take part occasionally. "Brag" and "Nap" were the particular favourites. With much humour would he relate to me how he "out-bragged young Tom Saunders" on a weak hand, or how he forced up the bragging with certain others, when he himself held a "Prail of Aces" which is incidentally the strongest possible hand.

Had he been spared Fred would have made his mark with this firm. In fact, without exaggeration I think I may say I think he would have done this anywhere for he was always so thorough, persevering and neat, and withal so genial and honest.

When about 16 years of age Fred joined the Young Men's Club at St Mary's Church, Plaistow, which had just been formed. Many were the pleasant evenings he and I spent there. In that club he was about the best billiard player and was easily the most skilful at that famous game "ping-pong". What tussles at these games we used to have and how often he has let me win a game just to encourage me. Draughts was a game, however, at which I could beat him, and to the draught board I would lead him when I wished to secure a sweet revenge for any particularly bitter defeat at "ping-pong". On reaching the age of 18, we were allowed to transfer our membership to the Men's Club. Needless to say, such an opportunity to become known as men was not to be missed and therefore as soon as eligible, we became fully fledged members of St. Mary's Men's Friendly Society. From that date until he left England, Fred was a member and a constant visitor to this fine institution. He really did appreciate the benefits to be had there. Innumerable incidents I could relate regarding things that occurred in that club room in which Fred played a part. Every member was his friend, as he was the friend of every member. Many of these members, his friends, have made with him "the great sacrifice".

Frequent billiard duels had Fred and I together. Later on we arranged a series of different games, including dominoes, bagatelle and draughts. We used to keep a careful record of these results and gain such fun from the frequent variation therein. How I would crow when I was on top, and how he would quietly "pull my leg" when he displaced me, which was very often. Those at home used to get quite interested in our club room battles. Many an evening have we spent together there, playing game after game, always in the best possible spirit.

Nobody ever knew him lose his temper at any game, or ever give up trying to win, however he was placed. Let me relate an incident to illustrate this. In a certain competition he had to play Mr Otto, the billiard champion. Fred had a long start, I believe, which his opponent soon almost wiped off. With about one hundred to go however, Fred proceeded to put together his record break. Quite a crowd of onlookers were there and the excitement was intense. He was perhaps the coolest there and just calmly walked round the table knocking the balls in his own methodical and careful way until he had made a break of 46.

Eventually he "ran out" an easy winner, but he was not a bit excited. In the final of the same competition he met his brother Frank. Despite the latter's superior skill he can bear witness what a struggle he had to defeat cool headed "sporty" Fred. A "sport", that is what Fred was. Cheating he abhorred, always he played and fought fairly and cleanly, just as he lived his life honestly and decently. Besides the games at the club, I can recollect the meetings of "young bachelors" generally in some quiet corner. Here they congregated for a smoke and a talk. Their conversation consisted generally of sport, politics or anecdotes, the last named predominating, judging from the frequent bursts of laughter that arose. The champion laughter at these little talks was Ronald Johnston – a great favourite with Fred. What sympathy this friend felt and what he thought of Fred can easily be judged by the following extract from his letter of condolence.

"He was a good friend to me and I thought to write you and say how very sorry indeed I am. Your boy lived a good life and then gave it nobly in the service of his country; he has gone with the fighters for freedom".

For several years Fred played splendidly in the football team, representing the Men's Club. It was in one of these games that he eventually met with the accident to his knee that precluded for always further active part in the football field. Before this had happened, however, he had won many games for the team by his skilful and vigorous play. Often he has so harassed his opponents that in desperation, they have resorted to fouling tactics to stop him, seldom with success however. Despite such unsportsmanlike opposition, I have never seen him commit other than technical fouls or ever take part in any "dirty" play. Before he was incapacitated, Fred was invited to play for the West Ham United reserves. He represented them in several matches during a Christmas holiday. I believe however, he did not enjoy these games very much owing to the lack of comradeship in the team, and to the roughness of the professional style of play at that period. Nevertheless as we watched his exhibition on the ground at the Boleyn can vouch he played by no means badly. He was always shy, however, and the fact of playing before a large crowd, so many of whom he knew, prevented his playing with all his accustomed skill.

Annually the church held some sports at a carnival known as the village fete. For quite a few years, Fred made it a practice to win prizes at these sports. Despite his sporting prowess, he was never heard to boast. If he won it was just good luck, if he lost it was just because the other fellow was the better man.

As I have intimated, Fred was a great favourite at the club. Let me illustrate this by a sentence or two from a letter of condolence received from another club member – Corporal Bailey.

"I shall always think of Fred as I always used to see him with a smile for everybody, he was one of the best fellows I ever came in contact with". Yes, that was it, a smile for everybody. Where an ordinary person would have found cause for losing his temper, Fred would just shrug his shoulders and smile, and such a fascinating smile too. I do not think I ever saw him really lose his temper. I cannot remember his ever having a bout of fisticuffs in anger, even as a boy at school. But had the necessity ever arisen, I guess he could have used nature's weapons very effectively. Somehow, such was his disposition, this necessity never did seem as though it would ever arise."

As in almost all English homes Christmas for us at Plaistow Park Road is a time of reuniting the family ties and for merrymaking and general enjoyment.

Wonderfully happy gatherings we have had in the past. Proceeding Christmas for several evenings a party of friends in the neighbourhood would fare forth into the night on carol singing intent. Incidentally a few collecting boxes were always taken along and the gleanings from these afterwards provided many soup dinners for poor children. Generally the carol choir consisted of about 30 happy girls and fellows. What melody used to rise on the chilly night from their willing throats. Fred was always an enthusiastic member of the party. How well can I recall a particular evening some ten years ago. It was Xmas eve, glorious with a full moon, frosty and clear. Round the harmonium which was our orchestra, gathered the choir. Cycle lamps acted as our illumination. Fred was with Ronald Johnston and Bert North, singing lustily but always melodiously. Real music it was that greeted the eager ears of those listening friends, cosily in their beds, but always appreciative of our efforts. All through the evening and early morning hours would the carollers continue to sing the "glad tidings" of Xmas until at 5 a.m. they would wend their way to St. Mary's Church, there to celebrate early communion.

Christmas day would pass, as it seems now, in a continuous round of fun and feasting. To give the ladies sufficient room to prepare dinner, we male members used to go and see a football match, Fred as always an enthusiastic unit of this party. Our return from what was very often a very cold watching of an unexciting game, was followed by Christmas dinner – and what a dinner. Defeat of our favourite team would not spoil even Dad's appetite and appreciation of Ma's faultless cooking. Dinner finished, with a very comfortable feeling beneath our waistcoats, to our cosy armchairs we would then repair. Yarns, funny and serious, anecdotes, true and fictitious, used to follow in rapid succession, and while the men enjoyed cigarettes or cigars, often supplied from the bountiful store, constituting a portion of Fred's "Christmas box". Like myself, Fred made a good audience on these occasions. A dry chuckle would mark his appreciation of one of Dad's old "chestnuts" while by a broad grin would he mark his approval of a witty sally by Fred Vowles.

Evening would see much preparation on my part to prepare some games and simple feats of conjuring. How Fred would "pull my leg" at my efforts in his direction. Perhaps I would ask him to assist me in some little matter connected therewith, how he would joke about it, and then at the crucial moment, let me down. Then he would laugh at me, while I taking pleasure seriously became annoyed. Then our games or cards in the small hours of the morning. I believe he often used to make mistakes purposely just to annoy Frank and Dad and cause some fun. In this he invariably succeeded, but really nobody could ever get angry with him. Then following our little card party, we would all go to bed. There he and I would lay talking over the wonderful doings of the day.

In accordance with arrangements made before retiring, the male members of the house would rise early next morning and taking advantage of the adjacent field, exercise their limbs and digestive organs by chasing an elusive football. Those were enjoyable days indeed. Dad would often come with us to watch and criticise and even join our game. How we boys would vie with each other to gain his praise. I do not think that any of those that used to take part in those games will forget them. There was enthusiastic F.H.C. vigorous Jack R, active F.J.V., amusing W.J.C., eager F.W.C., skilful Fred, and anxious to show off P.L.C.

What melees there used to be among the stones and rank grass of that useful field. Following these games, we would return for a breakfast, and then run and frolic until the holiday came to its rapid close.

What a boy Fred was for his home. Given a book and his pipe, a cheery fire and that big armchair, it would take much to coax him out during the long winter evenings. He would perhaps walk across and have a game of billiards and a chat then back he would come to keep dear Mother company. Often he would ask Mother if she would be alone for the evening. Should such be the case out would come his pipe and book, and he would cheerily compose himself by the fireside for the evening. There he would read while Ma sat with her little task of needlework or crocheting. Occasionally he would make some whimsical remark or Ma would ask him some question possibly as to what has happened that day at work. I have seen Fred reading, suddenly drop his book on his knees and sit biting his nails in his inimitable way just looking lovingly at Ma. How he did love her and Dad, only they can know. I wonder how many fellows would sacrifice their evenings just sitting with their mothers to keep them company. To him it was no sacrifice, although oftimes he would give up other pleasures so that Ma might have his company. It was one of his many "labours of love". Only Ma can know what the remembrance of these evenings means to her now.

Fred was very fond of walking with his friend George Hain, and would think nothing of covering a dozen miles during the evening. On Sunday mornings I can recall many occasions upon which in their company, I have been for splendid rambles round the lakes of Wanstead or through the leafy lanes of Barkingside. Girls troubled him very little. I do not think he ever met anybody he would have wished to marry, even if he had done so, I am firmly convinced he would have sacrificed his personal wishes, for he vowed that while Dad and Ma lived, he would remain single. Do not imagine however that he was anything of a woman hater. On the contrary, he was fond of the ladies' company, but never took them seriously. Many girls he has met and walked with and I feel confident that many of these would have much liked him to do what he never did with any one of them – fall in love.

Occasionally he would visit a music hall or attend some business function in the form of a dinner and concert. Well I recollect one of the latter occasions Fred had been out with Dad to an annual dinner – I just forget which particular one it was. At about 12.50 a.m. they returned. I had been in bed several hours. Fred's entry into the bedroom awakened me, which is not surprising, as he was falling and stumbling against different articles of furniture. At first I could not quite make out what was wrong. After such effort and wasted matches he managed to light a candle. Then he stood in front of the looking glass and made a little speech to his reflection therein. How clearly I remember the trend of his remarks, they were to the effect that a certain George Saunders was a very decent fellow. His words were pronounced in a curiously muddled way and presently the reason dawned on me, dear old Fred had taken more liquid refreshment than was good for him. I was about 18 years of age at the time. Fred was my pattern and my ideal of what a man should be. My horror to see him like this was intense. Up out of bed I jumped and ran straight down to Father's room. He can tell how Fred followed me into the room, how I said Dad should be ashamed of himself for not looking after Fred more carefully, how that dear fellow endeavoured to protest his perfect sobriety and finally how I told Dad and Ma I was sure Fred was not sober and then fled sobbing from the room. After that Fred was very unwell and I recall feeling an unkind delight in this fact, and thinking that it would do him good. And such proved to be the case. Never again did Fred take too much to drink. Very shamefacedly he carefully explained to me next day that he had very foolishly done what is known as "mixed his drinks". Until this incident, I do not think that I realised what Fred meant to me, in fact I do not think I ever did until that morning in August, years later, when the awful news was told me.

When Fred left Balaam Street School, I think he was just 14-years-old. The fact that he was so keen to earn his own living probably accounts for his not completing his education at a secondary school. Being desirous however, of adding to his knowledge in certain directions, he determined to attend evening classes. For three or four years he spent evenings each week at the West Ham Technical Institute. In his own plodding thorough way, he mastered the intricates of book-keeping and the monoronany of shorthand. As an example of this I would say that he succeeded in obtaining the Society of Arts certificate in the advanced stage for book-keeping. Further he covered many sheets of paper with machine and other drawings. This latter was more in the form of recreation for he was always fond of sketching and drawing. As a lad of about 18, he copied splendidly a print from a daily paper of the Duchess of Gainsborough. This and certain other sketches of his have been framed and form interesting relics of his activities in the world of art.

Everybody who knew him will recall that wonderful trait of neatness and tidiness that was his. He hated to be in a room which was untidy. He was never otherwise than neatly attired. Many times have I seen him set to work to put straight a room which did not happen to suit his discriminating taste in tidiness. This feature of his character, and also his love for home, accounted for the work he would do in the house and the trouble he would go to in order to obtain different things for carrying out little home improvements, and nothing would give him more pleasure than to carry out these little improvements himself whenever possible.

Photography was a hobby of mine. Incidentally it provided Fred with such amusement. Such droll remarks would he make about my partiality for spending a glorious evening in a stuffy dark-room. Only about twice did I manage to persuade him to let me take his photo, and then what a hunt I had. Getting him settled in a certain position I would proceed to arrange the camera. Presently I would look up to find him wandering about the garden – which was my studio. Then again would the hunt and arranging have to be carried through. One particular Sunday I think it was the best part of an hour before I succeeded in taking his portrait. Glad indeed now am I that I persevered in spite of – or perhaps because of – his "leg pulling", for that camera has given us a real likeness – just as we all knew and loved him in years before the great war.

Nobody who was of the party will forget the last holiday Fred had. It was at Minehead in Somerset. With him were Mother and Father and others making up a happy party of eight or ten. Unfortunately I could not go with them. It was during the splendid summer of 1914, just prior to the outbreak of the war, that this happy company spent what all afterwards voted was one of the best holidays in their lives. Many amusing anecdotes were related when they returned. One in connection with Fred and a certain American lady whom he encountered in the Doone Valley. Fred made some remark to this lady regarding the fact she had no coat. How well he mimicked her Yankee intonation in her retort that she would "sooner freeze than carry a coat". Fred declared that this lady was a real "sport" so she must have been. Other incidents relate to the manner in which he would often disappear when the party was out walking. As his companion was always a young lady named Doris, it can be understood that he had to put up with some banter from the others. He enjoyed this holiday wonderfully and often since referred to it with evident pleasure and anticipation of having similar holidays after the war. It has been ordained otherwise however.

End of Part One

- : -: -: -: - : -: -: -:- : -: -: -:- : -: -: -:- : -: -: -:- : -: -: -:- : -: -: -: - : -: -: -:

- : -: -: -:

PART TWO

SOLDIER

AS all the world knows only too well the great war began for Britain on August 4th, 1914. From that day until he enlisted at the beginning of November, Fred was very unsettled. At the very commencement he wanted to enlist. It happened I was rejected early in September and I could not but see that he was glad such was the case. He said, "Now you are not to try again old boy". Then just a few weeks later, during which time he was occupied in calming Mother's fears, he went with George Cunningham and enlisted in a London regiment, the 2/4th Royal Fusiliers. Directly he was in the army he was emphatic in his requests, and which almost amounted to orders – that I was to stay at home and look after the old people, as he so affectionately termed Ma and Dad. Always he thought of them and the worry his absence and danger would cause them, never did he consider the hardship and discomfort this same absence and danger would mean for him.

As usual he saw the humorous side of the uncomfortable period of training. He would never come home without some little anecdote of the peculiarities of army life. Rations were bad – he would not grumble. Rations were good, then he would remark the fact. Of course he made a smart soldier – it was always in him, the alertness and tidiness combined with the common sense that is necessary in the perfect infantrymen. All too soon was the training completed. After a few days in London he was sent with a draft to Maidstone. Here he seems to have had a good time. Dad paid him several visits and took him along to the house of a friend of his, resident in the town. I believe afterwards Fred was always a welcome visitor there. I must not omit the incidents relative to the fitting out of our "soldier lad", in his uniform and equipment. It was a Sunday evening when he came home bringing a kit bag full of the outfit the Government had issued to him. Upstairs he went. Half an hour passed and then he appeared among us who sat in the front sitting room. And what a droll object he did look to be sure.

His trousers were too small at the thighs by inches and too long in the leg by the feet. His coat fitted him but only where it touched him. I do not even think his cap was as it should have been. How I did laugh at him, and how he did laugh at himself. Ma immediately got her workbox and commenced to make his things more as they should be. Bits cut off here, stitches altered there, buttons moved to give more room, and presently the things were ready for him. Once more he garbed himself in the khaki and this time he did indeed look a soldier – if a new one. How proud we all were of him – and how this pride never did nor never will diminish. Often afterwards we talked and laughed over the curious figure he cut when first he donned the uniform that meant so much to him.

Within three weeks of his joining up he was home on that leave that is so dreaded but which means so much – the final four days. In his case it was but two days and a half. There is no need for us to mention the way he was fated during this all too short period. It was a Saturday evening of early December when he left home, little did he or we then think it would be over two years before he was to see his home again. Little did we know what he would have to endure. Little did I think that never again should he and I be together in dear old drab Plaistow and our "Domum dulci domum". A party of us went with him to Victoria – consisting of Dad, Grace, Nelly, Fred and myself. At Plaistow station we were joined by Arthur Cunnington who was accompanying his brother George. I can now picture those two brothers sitting in that train together. Such fine fellows they were. For many years Fred and I had known them as comrades. George was to journey, a soldier, with Fred. Arthur remained behind – a civilian for a short few months longer, like myself. How awful it is to think that both these strong healthy brothers, then as happy and contented, have since died on a bloody battle field of France.

What a crowd of departing soldiers we found at Victoria, and what partings we witnessed. Some were never again to see those dear ones left behind – but all were brave as they left those dear ones. I recall how we shook Fred's hand, how the girls kissed and hugged him. Not an emotion was apparent as he bade us goodbye – but just that clenching of teeth that was a habit of his and a steadfast look that betrayed feelings under control. Then away he walked, erect and steady despite unaccustomed pack and equipment. We tried to catch his eye should he turn his head. However, he never gave so much as a glance round – probably he feared to show his feelings he wished to hide. Always was Fred a boy who hated emotion and display of feelings. But none the less were those emotions and feelings deep and sincere within him, who would doubt who knew him well.

Once more 'ere he left England did Dad manage to see him at Maidstone, and I can imagine better than I can describe just what that meeting and parting must have been. It was the middle of December when Fred left Southampton, the destination being Malta. The passage was a very rough one; the boat was crowded and the food was bad, but one good thing was, enthusiasm of the "cause". Better than I can recall the facts will his letters to Ma – so treasured – describe the various stages of his army life before he came to France. My memory from reading these letters retains some outstanding facts that I will endeavour to relate. First however mentioning with what eagerness and interest his correspondence was always awaited and read by those at home.

His voyage to Malta was only half the novelty to him on account of his having some few years before made a trip to Lisbon and spent a week or so in that vicinity with Dad. Across the Bay of Biscay and the scenes on board according to Fred, were indescribable for the troops were crowded and most of them very bad sailors. However on entering the Mediterranean there was compensation. The boat skirted the coast of Algeria and Morocco and the scenery was gorgeous. For hour after hour in glorious weather they ran by wonderful sea scapes of which homely British tommies who lined the sides of the ship had only read or dreamed. A few days more and Fred found himself on the island of Malta – Britain's Mediterranean Sentinel. Here he was destined to remain for several months, learning with his comrades that military training necessary for the great struggle into which they were to be thrown. Squad drill, rifle drill, route marches, manoeuvres – though the whole gamut of different phases in learning to be a soldier did Fred go with his usual precision and thoroughness. His home was the barrack room, his food the army food. Of the former he once wrote telling me how during a certain night an individual who must have been a thorough rogue, robbed every fellow in his room while they slept. In that letter he just asked for some money to be sent out because he had just been relieved of about £4 by this thief. There was no complaint for himself but he felt bitter against the thief because he had robbed fellows who had but little money and were in poor circumstances at home. Regarding the food he had Fred would say very little but I do not believe he found it very appetising. He abhorred cheese as we all know and you can therefore imagine his feelings when he learned the menu for breakfast would always consist of cocoa and bread and cheese. I think he managed to do without the cheese and buy goat's butter. During his army life he tasted cheese only once and that was many months later in France. That cheese was baked and spread on bread. After much coaxing he was persuaded to try it. In confidence he afterwards told me it was not so bad but he did not think he could get to like it.

Malta, the land of bells, yells and smells as Fred once wrote, he found very beautiful from many points of view. The goats with the faces of bearded old men used to make him laugh. He visited many of the wonderful churches on the island and wrote home interesting descriptions of them. There was a droll miniature railway upon which they used to travel to the town of Valitta. In his usual generous way he sent home presents to mother – presents which will always be treasured. Amongst these was a beautiful piece of Maltese lace, watching the making of this he found very interesting. It was at Valitta he had his photo taken in his military attire. How delighted we were to have copies of this. Later on he sent several snapshots of he and his comrades disporting themselves on the sands and in the water. It was while having a bathe that he was badly bitten on the foot by a denizen of the deep. He was ill for about a week or two, but never a word to Mother for fear of causing her worry. This fact was only discovered afterwards by accident. There was a period of several weeks when he was one of the guard which was posted on the sea shore. This he said was a fine holiday, the only drawback being that they used to walk several miles for food and water. I believe his first night on guard in Malta found him posted as sentry in a cemetery and I think this was for him rather a weird experience. As the training drew near its completion, the battalion was taken out for a day and a night route march in full pack. One such march was so exhausting that only 12 of the whole regiment returned to headquarters to time. Fred was one of these I believe.

It was on the island of Malta that Fred spent the first Christmas of his life away from home. From his letters he did not appear to be unhappy but I well recall how we missed him at home. What parcels were sent off to him only Mother and his sisters can say. And how he did appreciate anything that he received in this way. I can recollect that my present to him was a letter of about 30 pages. In it I attempted to describe the happenings at 8, Plaistow Park Road during the Christmas festivities. He was very grateful for this, because it helped him to recall "home sweet home".

As the winter of 1915 drew to its close the training of Fred's battalion was completed, and in the early spring the regiment embarked and was taken to Egypt. For several weeks the troops were encamped in the desert near Alexandria. In a letter he said they were living on sand, sand was everywhere. When they ate anything it was permeated with sand, when they slept sand got into their eyes and ears, their mouths, their noses; and when they were awake sand blew up their sleeves and down their necks. In fact, everything was sand, but this they treated as a joke.

The monotony of this life was broken for Fred by visits he was able to pay to a friend of father's, a Mr Spurgen, who lived in Alexandria. Here he was treated as one of the family. His letters home indicated the enjoyment he derived from these visits.

The homeliness recalled his own home and those days before the war. Nobody can realise what these hours spent in an Englishman's home and with an Englishman's family meant to Fred who, always such a lover of home life had for months lived the hard and comfortless life necessary under army conditions. For their part, Mr Spurgen, his wife and daughter looked on him as one of their family and loved him as such. The news of Fred's death deeply affected them, and the following extract from their letter of condolence indicates once again the respect and love our boy always inspired wherever he went.

"We were very cut up at the bad news that our dear boy Fred is no more. We call him our dear boy for as I have said before he was one of the very best, how he used to talk and enjoy the evening with us. We shall never forget him. He was a most loving boy and his honest face would carry him anywhere and he would be loved by all. You have the knowledge he was loved by all and died for his "King and country". His thoughts were always for you all and his dear home. We feel it as if he was our own boy".

Occasionally parties from his battalion were allowed to go on excursions to various places of interest in the vicinity. One such outing was the world renowned pyramids and sphinx of Giza. Here after a long railway journey through the strange scenery of the East, the party spent several hours exploring those creations of a wonderful people. Fred wrote a really wonderful description of this outing telling of the pleasures he derived and the impression his mind received while being guided among such marvels of engineering. Further he described in detail all he saw on the journey and during the tour of the wonders of the world. Such were the merits of his description letter that Father had it printed so that it remains a memento to the powers of observation and description that our boy possessed.

On another occasion Fred wrote of a visit he and some comrades paid to a certain native village. His reference to the odours and the quietness of things in general was very amusing and striking. Evidently they found the smells striking too for in the end they were forced to leave the place on that account. He further stated that the village seemed as if it were a thousand years behind the times and the houses were hovels, the inhabitants were dirty, and, judging from a modern point of view, uncivilised.

Always were his letters very interesting and instructive, and indicated the observant way he went about, besides showing that he was deriving as much enjoyment as possible from the life he was leading.

All too soon were those weeks of comparative pleasure destined to come to an end. I think it was the beginning of June 1915, when Fred's battalion were transplanted to the Gallipoli peninsula. What horrors and hardships he underwent here, nobody will ever know exactly, for he was always reticent where his own doings were concerned. That he did undergo hardship and suffering of the severest is of course obvious, for later disclosures showed that not a soldier in the expedition but suffered and knew the pangs of hunger and thirst, and extremes of cold and heat; besides the hellish monotony of the trench life on that shell swept and barren strip of hard won soil is only too well known now. Never a complaint in letter afterwards, verbally did he make. He told me just a few incidents which are sidelights on his life during the six months or so that he existed on that peninsula. Once he said how he would take a tin of milk and making a hole in the top, drain the contents – that would sustain him for a day or so he said. Then again he has related how often a week or two without a wash or shave he managed to secure half a cigarette tin of dirty water. With this he would first shave and then wash, using his shaving brush as a sponge. There was one night when with a sergeant and another he was on patrol not many yards from the Turkish trenches. The sergeant, poor fellow, was shot through the head. They managed to get back to their lines but he died soon afterwards. There was a pain in Fred's voice when he told me of this incident – one of the very few relative to actual fighting he ever did tell me. Many a narrow escape he must have had during those weary weeks of burning heat and biting cold, but he would never allude to them for fear of causing anxiety at home. Even his reticence could not prevent him from alluding to an awful hurricane they experienced. He has since mentioned the awfulness of this. Many of the Turks were actually drowned in their trenches while a similar fate even befell some of his own comrades. The cold was intense. The wind terrible the rain, hail and snow awful. He said that was the worst experience he ever had. As we all know the expedition was a failure, and in January 1916, the troops were withdrawn. Fred's regiment was one of the last to leave the peninsula. He has told me that during the last week the troops were allowed to eat as much as they wished and they availed themselves of this permission to the full. Even then there were thousands of pounds worth of eatables destroyed, before the final evacuation. This fact, inevitable as it must have been, was very hard for those fine fellows to understand, for they had fasted and even almost starved for months, only to sacrifice the blood won soil and to see food which had been denied them wantonly destroyed. Of these facts Fred spoke to me afterwards and I believe even his wonderful endurance and patience was tried at this juncture although he would never admit it.

From Gallipoli the regiment went to the island of Lemnos to recuperate. Of this stay Fred had little to say. Truth to tell, I believe he was too exhausted to record his impressions and was just content to rest after the vigours of his first campaign.

After a few weeks on this island Fred's battalion were taken once more to Egypt. Here, being stationed close to Alexandria, he was able to renew his visits to Mr Spurgen and find a home occasionally for a few hours. Little as he wrote about such things, those homely hours must have been much for him after all he had recently experienced. On this occasion the regiment stayed in Egypt for about 10 weeks. During this time the troops were used for the purpose of intimidating the native population which showed some sign of unrest. This meant they marched through various villages parading the military might of Britain. During this period Fred must have seen much to interest him. On one such expedition it was that he met Joe Pett. It is much easier to imagine than to describe what such a meeting must have meant to them both. How long they were able to spend together I do not know, but it is easy to realise how much they had to say to each other and how little time was wasted. For details of exactly what occurred I must refer you to Joe who doubtless has mental notes of all the incidents.

While in Gallipoli all parcels were withheld from the troops so Fred did not receive any during that period. When, however, they arrived in Egypt there was a glut of parcels. Fred received about 14 in seven days. He has told me what feasts there were. Army rations were at a big discount and meals consisted of cakes and other "goodies" from dear old "Blighty". Cannot you picture dear old Fred opening a huge parcel from Mother. In it he finds one of those famous cakes. Out comes his hack knife, his friends first receive a big portion and then he himself settles down to enjoy his own share. And it is easy to guess of when and what he would be thinking while eating the cake. His mind would be doubtless back to those Sunday afternoons when such cakes formed an indispensible and invariable item of the menu; when everybody was at home, happy and comfortable; and when there was no war. Having enjoyed the cake and day dream he would then in all probability just shrug his shoulders and with a whimsical smile make some droll remarks to his comrades.

It was one day in April 1916, when I had been abroad just a few weeks, that news came to me that Fred was in France. He had made a most interesting journey through the whole length of the Mediterranean, then via Marseilles and the beauties of Southern France to Rouen. From here he wrote me a very interesting letter. He mentioned that before doing any more fighting he anticipated having leave. In the meantime they were allowed much freedom. He enjoyed fine walks in the vicinity of the town and spent many evenings at concerts and other entertainment provided for the troops. Moreover, he found much to interest him in studying the characteristics of French life. With their language he admitted he would never make headway; but this was chiefly because there was no necessity. After about a month in the city he and others were transferred from the 2/4 to 1/4 London Fusiliers and sent with a draft into the line. Fred did not say much but I know he felt bitterly the fact that having endured so much and been away from home for 18 months, leave was yet denied them. Furthermore, he was very sorry to leave his old regiment which was very dear to him. However, he realised that the necessities of war recognise no sentiment and just philosophically obeyed orders.

It must have been towards the end of May when he first went into the trenches in France which were held by the 58th Division, and for the rest of his military career his battalion served in this division. At that time I was stationed at a little village called Marieux. Fred and I corresponded regularly, but it was not until the middle of July that I discovered we had been for two months or more but eight miles apart.

In the meantime, however, much had happened. Fred had contracted septic heel and was sent to hospital. Here he remained for several weeks and returned to his unit on July 5th. While in hospital, by a marvellous coincidence, he once again met Joe Pett who had been wounded and incidentally had a narrow escape. Once again I can only refer to Joe for details of that meeting, which needless to say must have given great pleasure to both. A reference to the date of his return to the battalion on his recovery will indicate that Fred missed the "big push" of July 1st 1916. His comrades were in this and suffered rather heavily. Fortunate indeed did Fred consider himself to have been out of this attack.

It was a few days after his return that as a result of many enquiries I managed to trace my infantry brother. Let me tell you of this first meeting in detail. For days I had been seeking the whereabouts of his unit. It was July 14th when the much desired news reached me. As it happened I was off duty that day and was able at once to set out to trace him. At Souastic I was directed to Sailly-au-bois. On reaching the latter place I learned he had gone to Souastic for a bathe. Back I went and was just passing a group of infantry when a well known voice shouted "Hullo Perce". I looked round and there was dear old Fred just leaving the ranks, towel over his shoulder, and the happy smile on his face. Even as he walked those few steps I noticed the limp which indicated his foot was not quite better. What handshaking there was. Recollect it was 21 months since last I saw him and never before had we been apart more than a few weeks. Then think of all he had endured. I confess to a lump in the throat and even tears of happiness in my eyes. Try as he would, even strong Fred could not quite control his feelings. That grip of the hand meant much and I could feel the emotion in his voice as he spoke those first few words of pleasurable greetings. As it happened one of my tyres had sustained a puncture and so while I repaired it, Fred had his much needed bath, presently spick and span he appeared, just as neat and tidy as he always was. Our first business was to provide for the "inner man", it being well past time for dinner.

Away we went in search of the inevitable canteen. Here we purchased tinned fruit and biscuits. Then a walk in to a conveniently quiet meadow. This was the scene of those many picnics I was destined to have with the dear fellow in France. As it happened a parcel had recently arrived from home and I was able to augment the feast with some of Mother's famous cake. It would have done her good to see how we appreciated it. There we sat munching the good things in proper Bohemian fashion. Our fingers were the knives, spoons and forks, while the ground was our table. It was a glorious day and we were as happy as possible. Of the thousand and one things we talked about I must leave the reader to imagine. Dinner finished, Fred had to rejoin his comrades and march back to his dug-out at Sailly-au-bois. I preceded him on the motorbike and there awaited his coming. On arriving he conducted me to his temporary home. This was an old gun emplacement and to my critical eye a very uncomfortable place. Fred assured me, however, that it was a perfect home of rest. In a confined space of about 10 feet square, six men had to live. The beds were of wire netting stretched on wooden frames. Of course having beds at all was a luxury to those fellows, and one they appeared to appreciate, for whenever possible they seemed to be lying down on them. The remainder of the afternoon Fred and I spent in that billet. He introduced me to his comrades, most of whom had been with him to Gallipoli. It is sad to think that of those six fine fellows, but one is now alive – a lad named Mott. It can be understood that whenever the opportunity occurred Fred and I would be chatting of some of the many things that there were to talk about. At first it was of home and the dear ones there, then I tried to get him to tell me some of his experiences. This I found very difficult. Never would he talk freely of what he had seen and done, he was much too modest for that. It was fine to be with him, and to talk to him once more. It did me good who had left England recently, and it was plain to see how very delighted Fred was to meet someone from home after so many weary months of hardship and absence from home he loved so much. Though it is 16 months since that first never-to-be forgotten meeting I can picture clearly though it was but yesterday that happiness and pleasure in those keen grey eyes as he chatted with me that afternoon. We had so much to say that it was difficult to know what to say first. One interesting fact he mentioned was that for several days he had somehow been expecting to see me and had been scanning the faces of all passing motorcyclists; so while he was pleased, he was not so very surprised when he did see me. In due course tea was served in the fashion approved among the infantry. A huge "dixie" of tea was brought along by the cook's mate. From this a certain quantity was doled out into each man's mess tin. Then from different little store places each man brought forth that portion of his day's ration he had allotted for his tea. With his usual foresight Fred had economised and had quite a goodly store. I believe he used to affect this economy in case one day there would be no rations. I may here mention that on every occasion I saw Fred afterwards he always seemed to have more food in hand than his comrades. These latter seemed content to eat the whole day's ration at one sitting and fast for the remainder of the day. With the help of some more of Mother's famous cake, this time from a parcel Fred had received, we managed to make a splendid tea. Soon after this I had to return to Marieux for duty. With a hearty handshake I left him, promising that as soon as possible I would visit him again. He stood there as he always did, watching me until I was out of sight. It was just three mornings later that I was able to go over and see him once more. Unfortunately he was out, having been helping to dig a trench in front of Nebuterne during the night, from which duty he had not returned. There was not long to wait, however, a matter of an hour or so, then Fred appeared wearing tin hat and other implements necessary for such trench duties as he had been doing. Having worked most of the night and marched about 12 miles it can be imagined that he was rather tired. He was not too tired, however, to have a stroll and talk. He told me he had experienced rather an exciting few hours during the night. They were digging an advanced trench when "Fritz" began using trench mortar and machine guns. Several men were put out of action, and Fred himself had several narrow escapes. After that there was little work done.

At Marieux, being near a splendid little farm, I had been able to provide eggs and other little things for Fred, and on this occasion I brought some with me. He was as pleased as possible which more than repaid me for any little trouble I had been put to. In addition I brought him the body shield which Will had given to me and for which my duties found no necessity.

He promised he would always use this. As a matter of fact I discovered afterwards that after wearing it two or three times he found it too cumbersome and was forced to discard it. I believe he gave it to a friend of his. Twice more was I able to go and see Fred at Sailly-au-bois and on both occasions I managed to spend several hours with him. It was on the first of these two visits that he had a ride on my Triumph motorcycle. He was very interested and managed the machine quite easily although he was riding over rough ground. At the time I said how much I wished he had been a dispatch rider with me, and since then how many times have I again given expression to this wish. Before seeing him on the fourth and last time here I learned that my unit was to move on August the 1st. The last visit therefore was one of farewell. I managed to be with him from about midday until 7.00 p.m. We had much to say to each other and therefore went for a walk in the neighbouring fields. It must be remembered that this particular district had been heavily shelled. Sailly-au-bois was therefore a collection of battered and shattered walls. Hardly a roof was to be seen, fields had suffered and were scarred and torn by explosives. It was into one such field that we strolled to have our farewell chat. How distinctly I remember the incidents. There was a shell hole quite near, but where we sat the grass was rich and green. It happened that we were on a slight mound and were able to see across the war-racked countryside towards Nebuterene and the division lines. Even so close to the war zone an attempt at cultivation had been made and certain fields showed signs of ripening corn. On the whole however, the scene was one of desolation so peculiar to districts close to the lines. Despite the rather sad surroundings, our conversation was of the brightest. As always when we met we had such talk of home and the loved ones. There were incidents of our daily life to chat over, there was more to say than time would permit and although we had been lying there in the sun for several hours, talking almost incessantly, I can recall how surprised we were to learn it was time for my departure. I did not leave, however, before arrangements were made to meet again as soon as ever possible. Before we were able to see one another again months were to elapse and Fred was to see that dear home in England he loved so well. It was just getting dusk as I eventually left him on that evening of July 30th 1916. He stood there in that street of ruin on the little French village and watched me until I turned the distant corner. As I rode away my fingers tinged from that hearty grip of his, while in my mind's eye I carried a vision of his face tanned by the open air life and with those grey eyes of expression and affection. During these first visits to him I noticed how popular he was with his comrades. Only a private soldier but he seemed known to the whole battalion although comparatively new to it. His fellow inmates of that gun emplacement were sincerely fond of him. "The old man" they would affectionately call him. They would do many things to save him trouble. Wherever I have been and seen Fred with his popularity was a notable fact. Not a false popularity of a blustering bully but a popularity of one who by his whole demeanour and all his motions, by his sympathy and kindness to others, naturally gained the affectionate regard of his fellows. As in civil life there was never one to say aught against him, so I found it in his military life – for I went out of my way to discover this fact. Before leaving the incident of this period I must not omit to mention Lance Corporal Perndrille. He was in charge of that billet in which Fred lived. I found him to be an absolute Cockney – one of the humorous good natured sort. From him I learned how well Fred was liked. He himself was very fond of him. Although nominally in charge, I found he would always defer questions to Fred and act out his opinion. He had been through Gallipoli in the 2/4th London Fusiliers, and had known Fred the whole time since they left England. It was from him I learned that had Fred chosen he might have had promotion and become a sergeant many months before. On this point I tackled Fred one day and I learned that he had no ambition for promotion in the army. He was there to do as he was told and would do so; but he did not wish to be in a position which would force him to give orders to his old comrades. An unusual standpoint perhaps, but one which in that unassuming soldier brother, can be quite understood.

So we once again parted but this time only for a few months, and during these months we corresponded frequently. I can recollect that I had a shock when a letter I sent him in October was returned a few weeks later marked with that significant word "wounded". As it happened I had a letter but a day later from Fred himself, saying he was quite well. As this was anti-dated to the note on my returned letter I was much relieved; for having heard that the 56th division was in the "big push" on the Somme I had been very anxious on his account. As a matter of interest I sent that returned letter on to Fred and I believe he preserved the envelope as a souvenir.

Difficult as writing is in the trenches, he always found time to let me and those at home know, of his safety, even if it was only by sending a field postcard. For her part Mother treasured religiously any letter or card he sent. There was a book allotted specially to his letters and therein each day one found its resting place. I am afraid the rest was often disturbed, for Mother whenever opportunity occurred, would read and re-read these letters which are so precious to her.

It was towards the end of November when Fred's regiment were withdrawn from the Somme front. They had been in much heavy fighting and had sustained severe casualties. By much questioning I later managed to learn something of what they had experienced. The battalion was in the taking of some of the small but all important villages and woods that meant so much at that time. They were Bouliaux and Luise woods and the villages of Oinchy and Combles. As it happened Fred was once again fortunate enough to escape this heavy fighting.

Before going into the line he also with 15 others had been chosen as runners and being the eldest soldier he was put in charge of the remainder. Now as any infantryman will tell you, a runner's job is no sinecure. He has to keep up communication between the advancing troops and the battalion headquarters and had therefore often to pass through the enemy barrage fire. But being in charge Fred had to remain in battalion headquarters which was frequently in a safe dug-out. There was an occasion when he had a narrow escape, however. He had gone to a small dug-out wherein some of the runners took shelter to detail one of them off to take a message. Hardly had he left the place when a "minniwerfer" or German trench mortar shell pitched clean into it. The poor fellow he had just spoken to was killed while another runner who was also there was badly wounded. Calling for a stretcher bearer Fred ran back at once and commenced to bind up the wounds of the poor fellow who had been hurt. Only by much careful questioning did I manage to learn of this incident.

One of the hottest times he ever had was on an occasion when all the runners were temporarily sent back to the regiment for a certain attack. It appears the weather had been very bad and the ground was heavy. Mud and water were everywhere. At a given time the battalion was ordered to be at a certain spot to commence the attack. At this time our barrage opened but unfortunately the troops were some hundreds of yards behind their alloted positions. Directly our artillery put up a barrage, this intimating the attack is about to be made, the German artillery opens with a counter barrage on a spot more distant behind where the advancing troops should be. This is to prevent reserves being brought up, and is what occurred on the particular occasion referred to. As a consequence the German counter barrage fell right among Fred's battalion who were not in their correct position. He told me it was awful. Men fell in all directions. Realising what had happened the officers gave the order to take cover. Fred and several more found a shell hole full of water and mud. Here they remained for half an hour which seemed like an eternity. That night they found many a good comrade missing when the roll was called.

Fred once spoke to me of an advance after a particularly heavy bombardment by our artillery. Suddenly they came upon one of the famous German sunken roads, he said it was literally piled up with enemy dead and dying. Our guns must have concentrated on this road with awful precision and by chance caught and almost annihilated a column of German troops. Gruesome details of his personal encounters with the dead, and other awful horrors he would never relate. His anecdotes were few and always impersonal.

He hated the war and keenly sympathised with those of ours and even the enemy whom he saw suffering awful wounds patiently.

The second day after leaving the Somme trenches the battalion was to march 21 miles. Later on I learnt what the march must have meant to Fred. During the last few days in the line he had contracted boils and impetigo on his legs. He refused to see the doctor although he must have been in great pain. On the day in question he found it impossible to keep up with his comrades and after a few miles he had to drop in the rear. His officer trusting him to come on at his own pace. When I say that he marched 17 miles in full pack despite the conditions of his legs, only those who have suffered the complaints mentioned can realise what he endured, and his pluck and hardiness in keeping going. When he had covered that distance night fell and he could go no further. Finding a small hay-stack he climbed on to it. Digging a hole in the hay he covered himself with his overcoat and then ground sheet and as he told me slept like a top until about six o'clock next morning. Looking out of his burrow he discovered there was a thick white frost. He admitted to me it was very cold and he felt rather hungry. This is not surprising considering that he had subsisted on biscuits during the arduous previous day. However, he climbed down and once more set out. He did not manage to get very far for even his determination could not carry him on. As it happened he managed to reach a field ambulance and went in. Here he was treated with every kindness. On giving his name to a sergeant in the R.A.M.C. the latter asked him if he had a brother who was a teacher in West Ham. It proved to be Earwaker, a fellow student of mine at Russell Road Teacher's Centre. This sergeant saw Fred's legs were properly attended to and gave him a good meal. He wished Fred to stay and receive proper treatment for some days, but with his usual sense of duty the latter said he must push on and catch up with the regiment. So away he went, his perseverance was rewarded and he reached his comrades just as they were about to entrain for a northern destination. I believe his officer commended him for "sticking it" so well and told him to "go sick" when they detrained. This Fred did and spent a week or two in hospital until his legs were quite well.

When Fred related the above incidents to me – little by little and at different times – I thought of a certain occasion, perhaps a dozen years before, which equally illustrated his wonderful perseverance. That was when, having borrowed Father's heavy but reliable roadster cycle, he started out on a journey to Southend quite alone. Reaching Bread-and-Cheese Hill, three miles from Southend and 33 miles from home, he burst the back tyre. A cycle repairer to whom he took it declared the cover and tube ruined and irreparable. Without more ado Fred turned his face towards Plaistow and commenced to walk home. It was then 10 a.m. – at about 10 o'clock that evening came a knock at the door at home. Opening it disclosed poor Fred with Father's cycle. He was almost in a state of collapse when he got inside. The whole of the 33 miles he had walked and pushed that machine. Seated in the armchair in the kitchen he recounted his adventures, while he bathed his feet and mother prepared food for him. And what a state his feet were in, all swollen and blistered. Asked by Mother why he did not come back by train, he confessed he had spent most of his money on the outward journey in trying to quench a thirst induced by the heat of the day. When it was pointed out to him that he could have paid his fare later by giving his name and address, he admitted he had never thought about that. Imagine pushing a cycle 33 miles on a warm day with just a few sandwiches to eat. I always considered this was one of Fred's wonderful feats of endurance. We had to smile at him but I think we all admired his pluck and hardiness.

A few weeks after moving north Fred was granted leave. After over two years absence from England, years of danger and hardship, he certainly merited the holiday. It was not necessary for me to relate the incidents of those precious 10 days in England for all the details will be treasured in the memories of those at home. He was feted right royally. Need I speak of the joy of Mother and Father to have him with them again. There were parties and car rides, days of visiting and days of rest at home, with those he loved so well. In the St Mary's Men's Club he received quite an ovation. When he went to see his old colleagues of business days a wonderfully warm welcome awaited him. Wherever he went he was met with that treatment which could only indicate the affection and respect in which he was always held. Afterwards when I met him he was full of the kindness of all at home. For the first two or three days he said things seemed just a dream but during the last week he awoke to the reality and had a wonderfully enjoyable time.

The inevitable parting came at last and was endured as Britons have learned to endure such things, and once again Fred found himself in France.

Hardly had he been with his unit a few days after his return than an opportunity occurred for him to transfer into the Stokes Trench Mortar Battery. He availed himself of this and was sent for training to a village close to the town of Merville. Having written to me telling of this change I determined to see him, again quickly. I was able to trace his new unit quite easily. It was the Saturday after Christmas day, 1916 when I set out to find him. As it happened I was wrongly directed on several occasions and it was not until after midday that I found him. The billet was a barn by the side of that fine canal that runs through Merville. It was a cold damp day and the machine and myself were covered with mud when I rode up to his barn. Inquiring for Fred, I was met with the query "You're 'is brother, ain't yer?" thus indicating a likeness between us. They said Fred had just gone out and pointed to him walking by the canal a short distance away. Riding towards him I "tootled on the horn".

Looking round he at once saw who it was and literally ran towards me and nearly wrung my hand from my arm. Pleasure at seeing me was written all over his face. Taking me back to his billet he safely bestowed my motorcycle and kit. Then away we went towards Merville. As luck would have it I had brought with me the remnant of a Christmas parcel and we munched of this while we walked and talked. And he appreciated that cherry cake for while on leave and due to his transfer his parcel had gone astray. Along the tow path we strolled. This time it was he who had the latest news from home and he did not fail to give it to me in the minutest detail. He then went on to explain that the T.M.B. was "cushy" as he termed it. While the work was less arduous it was more interesting. Moreover, there was much less time to be spent in the trenches, thus proving it was a safer job. Of this latter fact he seemed more pleased on account of those at home than of his own sake. An additional advantage was that the food was much better in the new unit. All these advantages he impressed on me and asked me to impress on those at home, so keen was he to relieve their anxiety on his behalf. Chatting in this way we passed through the town, meeting and having a word on his way with Fred's old friend Corporal Pendrille. As it happens there was an inter-battalion football match during the afternoon and as his old battalion was playing, Fred suggested we should go and see the game. The ground was a quagmire and the Royal Fusiliers were defeated by six goals to one but those things did not worry us. We referred to other games we watched together back there at home on the Boleyn Ground. That led us to talk on many things connected with the pre-war life and I was afraid we did not pay much attention to the game. While leaving the ground afterwards Fred happened to see two of his old Gallipoli comrades. They had obtained commissions and were there in all the array of Sam Brownes and new officers' clothing. Nevertheless they beckoned Fred and had a few words with him. On his return I asked him why he did not apply for a commission. He quietly replied that he was quite content to be a private soldier and did not aspire to any higher position in the army.

In Merville there is a little café where for the magnificent sum of one and a half francs we could obtain steak and chips, bread and butter and coffee. To this place Fred and I and two of his comrades went directly after the football match. Here I aired my little knowledge of French, much to Fred's delight, and ordered all they could give us for the one and a half francs as above. And we found it good. True, the tablecloth was an absentee while the utensils were not too clean, but the "grub" was above suspicion. Appetites satisfied, I went to get my motorbike from the barn. Fred accompanied me and afterwards had a joy ride on the carrier at the back, to the town. Leaving machine and kit in a convenient back lane we then went to one of those innumerable cinemas provided for the amusement of the troops abroad. The hall was crowded and we were forced to take a seat in front among a batch of very talkative little French children. Moreover, to the best of my recollection the pictures were poor and the so called orchestra atrocious. Nevertheless Fred and I were perfectly happy for we were together once again. At about eight o'clock I left him with a promise to run down again as soon as possible.

It was three days later when I had an opportunity to again visit Merville. I found the billet was changed for a warmer barn. This was due to the weather which had been very cold. With two Scots chums "Kilties" we went into the town. Once more we refreshed ourselves with steak and chips. Then we adjourned to a café ostensibly to have a drink but really to sit down and warm ourselves by the fire. Well do I remember a remark by one of the "Scotties". He was sitting quite close to the fire and the heat had evidently aroused certain inhabitants in his clothing for he suddenly said with his droll Scots accent at the same time rubbing his shoulder: "Freddie, lad, there's a mass attack taking place in me rear". While this remark made me feel quite creepy, I had to laugh. As Fred and I had much to say to each other we shortly went for a walk through the town. Later on, when I went to get my machine, I found a tyre punctured. Fred was very concerned and did all he could to help me repair the damage. He was also very careful that I was warmly clad before I left, owing to the severity of the cold – considerate as always for others.

The next occasion I went to find him he had left Merville. Eventually I traced him to Leventre, a village hardly damaged although quite close to the trenches. He took me into a little shop where there was a French mademoiselle whom he called Alice. Here we had eggs and chips while Fred carried on an animated conversation with Alice in the wonderful English the French people have cultivated. As usual, stroll and talk followed and I learned some of his experiences in the trenches for the first time, with the Trench Mortar Battery. He voted it was good fun, much better than being in the infantry, but there was one occasion when they spent an uncomfortable few hours. That was when they had to stand ready one night for three hours without overcoats with the temperature at zero. This was the coldest spell he had ever experienced. As the night wore on it was "proposed and seconded" that we visit a certain house for some chips and coffee. We did this and had a good feed. It will be noticed that when we met, Fred and I did not omit to look after the "inner man" however much we had to talk about. After this supper I went with him to his billet. This time it was a hut. Each man seemed to have a space 6ft by 16 ins. Comfort seemed to be at a discount, yet I heard not a single complaint. Unconsciously I compared the conditions under which Fred lived here to the conditions he so appreciated in his home and I began to realise something of the sacrifice he had so willingly made. We seated ourselves on his limited space and just chatted until it was time to leave. In the lane I again met those two Scots boys – fine big fellows they were too – with whom Fred was so friendly. "Uncle" they called him and respected him perhaps more than they would their own uncles.

Once more I saw "Uncle" before he was wounded. That was on February 4th. Unfortunately I had a difficulty in finding him on this occasion so that I was only able to spend half an hour with him.

As a matter of fact I nearly rode into the trenches in trying to trace his unit which was near Neuve Chappelle. They were in a huge barn, bare, battered and cold but the fellows all seemed quite happy. When I entered the place I can recollect there was a sing-song in progress. Fred I found in a corner writing home. We just went outside for a quiet chat. The weather was terribly cold and he told me they had found it stiff work in the trenches at night. He anticipated shortly going back near the town of Aire for training purposes.

As we all know this never materialised for on 7th March Fred was wounded near Neuve Chappelle. The news reached me on March 18th in a letter from himself in which he cheerfully wrote that he was having a fine time in the 20th General Hospital. Later on I heard details of what occurred. It seems that No. 4 section, 168 brigade T.M.B. – Fred's unit, were sent into the trenches to "send a few over to Fritz". As it happened Fritz resented this treatment and retaliated with missiles of all kinds. It was a shell of the shrapnel variety that burst over the crew of Fred's gun. The whole of the six men forming the crew were wounded but I believe he was hurt most severely. A splinter of shell hit a rib in his left side, which was severely bruised, and which deflected downwards into the diaphragm. It was a narrow escape for had the splinter deflected upwards it would have penetrated the heart. In addition a second piece passed under his chin and out through his coat collar at two places. Fred said when he "got it" the impression was as if somebody had hit him with a big hammer. Despite the wound he yet seemed to see the humorous side for he wrote of the different quaint expressions his five comrades made as each discovered he had been hit. On the whole these expressions seem to have been of a delight for the wounds meant a rest in dear old "Blighty". I learned from his comrades later that Fred refused a stretcher and walked down to the dressing station a mile or more distant. He was doubled up though, and on reaching there almost fainted. They say he made not a bit of fuss and nobody knew he had been hit until some little time after the others had proclaimed their hurts when he remarked that he thought something had struck him as well.

After many enquiries I learnt that the 80th General Hospital was at Caniceria, a little town on the coast. At about one o'clock on that fine but very cold Friday I managed to set out on that 80 mile ride to try to get a glimpse at my infantry brother. After a good run through fine country I reached Caniceria at about four o'clock. Impatiently I enquired for the particular ward and was taken to it by an orderly. Imagine my personal disappointment when after anxiously scanning the beds I learned from the nurse in charge that Private Cearns had gone to "Blighty" that very morning. But how glad I felt indeed for his sake, to know that once more would he see the loved ones at home and perhaps spend several months in his native country. The nurses were very kind and told me all they could of Fred. "Oh yes! I remember him," said one of them, "he was slightly bald, and so like you". Of course I mentioned my relationship. From further enquiries I learned to my delight that the wound was not dangerous, but would keep him in England for some time. The nurses told me how quiet and uncomplaining he was, never a grumble but always smiling and happy. After some further talk and a good tea which they thoughtfully provided I set out on the return journey. Despite the distance I felt well repaid to have learned what I had. My mind as I rode through the dark night pictured the joy at home to have Fred with them again and his happiness to be with them.

For just three months Fred was in England. Then he was sent out again to France; sent out before he was sufficiently recovered from his wound to carry his own pack, and having a piece of enemy shell still in his body. The news came to me while I was doing duty at a delightful spot on the northern coast of France. And the news was a blow for I had hoped that many months would elapse before the dear fellow would have to face the awful trench life again. If the news was hard for me, what a terrible thing must the parting have been for the dear ones at home who knew how really unfit Fred was to face active service and how unfairly he was being treated.

For a fortnight or more Fred was in a London hospital. Here after due examination it was decided to allow the splinter of shell to remain in his body owing to danger entailed in trying to extract it. In every possible way he met with kindness in hospital. There were various outings and visits to theatres, and in fact the treatment he received left nothing to be deserved. On every visiting day what a crowd there always was to see him, parents, sisters, brothers and friends. I can picture the look on dear Mother's face, the tears of gladness in her eyes as she turned down the ward to her boy on that first occasion. There was, I know, a desire on her part to shed a tear but some droll remark of Fred's prevented her doing so. Mother had expected to see Fred lying in bed and was very surprised when he walked down the ward to meet her, for he had made a rapid recovery up to a certain point. What happened at that first meeting in hospital is doubtless a sacred treasured memory now to Mother, but we can imagine much of what passed. Then dear Father, think of his handshake, the grip that conveyed so much, when first father and son met in the ward. There would be fond greetings followed by plain for the future and enquiries regarding the past. There would be the chatting over of the happy days before the war, perhaps of the holidays spent together in Somerset or Portugal. And then the sisters and brothers and friends, all equally glad to see their Fred back even if wounded. He never lacked company whenever visitors were allowed, of that I am certain.

When convalescent Fred was sent down to Eastbourne to that wonderful Sunnedown camp for convalescent soldiers, he was there for about six weeks – weeks of happiness and quiet rest. Kindly people invited him with others to tea while there were many motor trips through the surrounding country. One little fact which afterwards came to my knowledge was in connection with a darby shooting competition held in the camp. There was a daily prize of one shilling for the best exhibition of shooting during each day and a weekly prize of five shillings to the one who gained most of the daily prizes for the week. During the time he was there Fred won every day and of course every weekly prize. He laughingly told me of this later, treating the matter quite as a joke. Really though, he was a splendid shot and afterwards at the base camp at Havre had the best result in the battalion.

Firing 10 rounds in 50 seconds at 250 yards, he managed to get nine bulls while the next best had only seven. A friend of his named Webster told me of this incident.

All too soon for Fred I am sure his period of convalescence came to an end. The doctor at the camp at the time thought of extracting the splinter of shell but afterwards decided to abide by the decision of the London Hospital.

Following the weeks of happiness at Eastbourne there were 10 days of home leave granted to Fred. What days they must have been to him and all those at home, every moment filled with incidents now a treasured memory. The joys of his first leave from France were repeated with the added feeling of thankfulness of having passed through many more dangers and experienced further hardships he was yet alive and well except for the effects of the wound. As before he was feted everywhere. One of his employers, Mr Rihll, took him out for an evening and treated him quite like a friend. That Fred appreciated this fact is evident because afterwards he told me about it and remarked what a splendid time he had and how kindly the "boss" treated him. And so indeed he felt in regards to all the kindnesses that everybody showered upon him. He said it was wonderful the way Mother would wait on him and try and make him eat enough for four men and the girls be ready to carry out his slightest wish. Dear Dad too with his little yarns, the games at billiards and his affection, how lovingly he afterwards spoke of him and the times they spent together during those days. I picture one of the family gatherings in his honour and imagine him sitting there just listening and passing only an occasional remark. In his pleasure Fred was never boisterous and his happiness would just show itself in the expression on his face and in those steadfast grey eyes. Yes they were days of perfect happiness there in that Plaistow home, but days that flew by all too rapidly.

Fred duly reported himself on the conclusion of his 10 days' leave and was sent to Aldershot. That must have been the 20th May. Immediately on arriving he was examined by the doctor and classed A3, indicating fitness for active service.

Considering his condition this ruling was amazing and very unfair for he could not walk far and certainly could not march with a pack. Those at home were very disturbed at the doctor's decision while Fred himself, without saying much was evidently disappointed and surprised. He had suffered much hardship and danger and he must have felt in view of his condition that he would have been marked for home service. Had he ever been in B Class, through the medium of some good friends he could have obtained a transfer to a searchlight section in London. It was not to be, however, within a fortnight of going to the depo he was once more at Plaistow. This proved to be the last fatal four days' leave which were the last few days ever he would spend with those dear ones in his beloved home. Mother wrote to me telling how it was towards the end of the second day before she learned that it was final leave Fred was having. Something seemed to have told Mother this and she immediately questioned Fred. Eventually he admitted that soon he might be again going to France and in the same breath begged Mother not to worry or be anxious about him. But it was impossible for either Mother or any of the other dear ones to feel other than anxious and how terribly justified was their anxiety to prove. I am afraid those few days were hardly joyous ones. The girls and his brothers would I know do their best to make things more cheerful but their task must have been well nigh impossible. It seems Fred himself was very quiet and thoughtful – more so than usual. The frequent quiet joke and smile were missing. He must have felt the injustice with which he was being treated. Not a grumble not a complaint however did he give vent to. His sole thoughts were for his dear Mother and Father, that they should not worry about him. But I think his own quietness must have affected everybody, for all seem to have remarked it. Indeed it has been suggested, perhaps with truth, that dear Fred had some premonition of his approaching end. Never before had he seemed so loathe to leave home, never before so quiet and thoughtful. Later when I was on leave Dad quietly told me that somehow he did not think he should ever see Fred again on this earth. Mother told me how hard that last parting was for father and son. Imagine the feelings of a father, who shaking hands in a farewell grip with his son, feels certain he is looking for the last time on that son's face and, moreover feels that the son is going to meet his death in some awful manner that modern warfare entails. Such feelings must Father have experienced on that June day when Fred left home for ever. Imagine too what that dear fellow himself felt, trying to maintain a cheery manner, yet believing all the time that he was looking his last on those dear haunts of his youth and saying his last goodbye to his loved ones. Yet did the father shirk the sacrifice or the son his duty? No! Both realised the meaning of the call to duty. Despite the real injustice that was being done no complaint was by either he who was to give his son or he who was to give his life to the country in its hour of need.

During the fleeting hours of these last days it goes without saying that everything possible was done to cheer and comfort our dear soldier boy. He paid a hurried visit to the circle of his friends and I warrant that those he encountered will always think of him as they last saw him, wounded and not yet fit, but bravely prepared to go and add to the "bit" he had already done for England's honour and our safety. I guarantee heavy at heart though he was he had a cheery word and ever a droll joke to crack with his old friends at the works and in the Club.

As I myself experienced it, so can I picture that scene of parting outside the house, but how necessarily more serious the faces then; for he was bound for the trenches while fortunately I was destined to serve miles behind the lines. There they are, that wonderful mother and father, these sweet sisters and brothers at the old iron gate of that dear home. Will's car awaits the hero. In the midst of the little group he stands. He has kissed his sisters, shaken hands with his brothers and friends; then with a long and fond embrace he leaves mother and finally grasps the hand of father. They took a deep look into one another's eyes and souls, perhaps both knew they were parting for ever on this earth but there is no hint of such feeling, just a manly grip and then into the car he jumps. Mother runs forward for one more kiss, the last she would ever give that splendid son of hers. Then away he goes. About to round the distant corner he looks round and waves his hand to the watching saddened group – and so they look their last on that wonderful son, brother, and he that hero, looks his earthly last on them.

News reached me on June 16th in a letter from Fred telling me he was at La Havre. At that time I was on duty near Calais and intended running down to see him until I discovered the distance was about 180 miles which made it impossible. Letters passed between us continually however, and I learned that towards the end of June he was sent up the line with a draft. His regiment was at that time the 1/3rd London Fusiliers who were however serving with his old battalion in the 56th division. As it happens some of his old friends of the 1/4th were in the draft so that when he reached his unit he was not quite amongst strangers. He was sent down towards Arras to join the battalion, but almost immediately the division moved north and to the rear. Their destination was the tiny village of Serques not far from St Omer.

In the meantime I had been home and had learned of what has been related in these pages. Further as stated, dear Father confided in me his fears that Fred had left him forever on earth. Try as I would to disabuse his mind of such ideas, somehow his conviction was so great it had an effect on my feelings. A similar premonition seems to have been sent to Will for he mentioned to Jessie, his wife, that he doubted if ever he should see Fred again this side of the grave. One cannot but wonder if these forebodings are not sent on order that the mind should in a measure become accustomed to the idea of the coming blow and loss.

Just two weeks after my return to France after leave I learned that Fred's division was about 25 miles distant. On Saturday July 28th I set out to trace him. From village to village I was able to trace the battalion until at last at Singnes I found it and him. Just as I was entering the village I rode by a column of troops on the march. I learned it was the 1/3rd London Fusiliers. Imagine how carefully I scanned the faces as I slowly rode by. As it happened, however, I was unable to see the boy. His platoon billet was pointed out to me and I eagerly rode towards it. A decent fellow – a thorough Cockney went to find him for me. Circumstances destined that this same fellow should be one of those to break the awful news to me within a few short weeks. A few minutes elapsed and there Fred came. With that grip of the hand and a few cheery words he greeted me. He did not say much but his looks were eloquent. The sweat was pouring from him for they had just marched a dozen miles and after his months in England he was out of training. He took me to his sleeping place under a tree in a fresh meadow. Here he lived with three others, his friends. There was an army dinner of stew and biscuits served up but we did not avail ourselves of that as there was the remains of a parcel of Fred's to finish, and some cake I had brought with me. Then the canteen supplied us with some tinned fruit for dessert. That afternoon we sat chatting and on this occasion it was I who had the news to tell from home. Eagerly he asked if Mother and Father were looking quite well and keeping cheery. In fact, he wanted to know everything I did during my leave. Fred looked quite well but perhaps not quite so stout as when we last met. Really after what he experienced I was surprised to find him in such good health and spirits. On my asking him to do so he showed me the scar of his wound – so small but which might easily have proved fatal. I learned that he felt only an occasional twinge from the splinter of shell he still had in his body; but to me it seemed difficult to understand why the authorities should have found it necessary to send out to the trenches one who had done so much and was still suffering from the effects of a wound received in his country's defence.

Not that the lad complained to me at all, he seemed quite contented and almost happy if just a little quiet. With pleasure he told me that soon he anticipated being transferred back to the old trench Mortar. The battery O.C. had been asking for him and promised that he would affect the change as soon as possible. Then again, that very morning his Colonel – a fine man named Soloman – had asked him what the grenade sign was on his tunic. On being told that it signified Stokes T.M.B. man, he enquired if Fred would like to go back to the battery and was of course answered in the affirmative. Thus the dear fellow was eagerly looking forward to soon being with his old friends.

As a matter of fact that evening I went to find the location of the 168 T.M.B. so that he could pay them a visit later. Luckily I discovered that it was quite near at hand. In the meantime I had learned five comrades, the names of two of them I remember were Webster and Worth. We had a picnic there together 'al-fresco' beneath that tree in the meadow adjoining an apple orchard. (Although the apples were not ripe the boys were busy knocking these down and munching them.)

I think you can picture the scene there on that summer day. Army rations we had augmented with tinned salmon and sardines, and we had quite a feast for there was more of Mother's cake available as well. We sat round, a groundsheet as our tablecloth, chatting and eating contentedly. They were all quite happy and glad to have a rest after their journey from the Arras district. The prospect before them, for they knew they were training for the big push at Ypres, did not seem to dismay them at all.

That evening after I had made the little journey referred to above, we went for a walk into the little village. It was rather a miserable little place but that did not affect us as we chatted of the things nearest our hearts. Strangely enough a letter I had sent him reached Fred after I met him that day. In it I had told him of the good time I had spent at home on leave.

At about eight o'clock we returned to the bivouac and just sat and talked and smoked until it became dark. Having arranged to stay the night I was to share Fred's bed, and what a bed this proved. There were no blankets but just one groundsheet and Fred's overcoat and the hard ground. Nevertheless after much manoeuvring we managed to both get beneath the overcoat. Of course there was no question of removing ones clothes. There we lay, Fred and I beneath the starry heavens. For a time we talked and then we were silent. I did not get to sleep for a long time and neither did Fred. I believe, like myself, he was possibly thinking of other times and circumstances. My mind went back to when he and I last shared a bed there in that cosy top room at home, that room where we had passed so many hours alone together and which had seen so many of our boyish pranks and exchanges of confidences. Almost three years had elapsed since then – years fraught with such danger and hardship as will never be known for that brother lying at my side. I cannot write of my feelings of happiness to be once more with him and to share again his bed, simple as it was. With his last words he had asked me if I were quite comfortable and warm, then he had given me some more overcoat. Beneath that tree sacred to my memory now, as sheltering our last resting place here on earth together.

I lay gazing at the stars and just thinking. But my thoughts never were of that which was to happen, only of happiness to have found him and to be with him once again. I will confess that tears came into my eyes as these things crossed my mind and as memories of home, of Mother and Father, of sisters and brothers came to me. Presently I fell asleep, his arm embracing me. The hard ground so comfortless to me was a bed to which he was well accustomed and so he slept well. When I found his arm thrown round me as if protecting, imagine my feelings – I cannot describe them.

Reveille next morning was at six o'clock. There was a red sky which pertained bad weather. This was only too well justified, for after breakfast it commenced to rain. Wrapping all the kit in waterproof sheets we returned to the shed wherein the others slept. For more than two hours we sat listening to some harrowing and some amusing yarns of experiences on the Somme and at Arras. Some of the most awful things I heard, of fighting and suffering and even cruelty. Occasionally humour would creep in from a tall Cockney with a wonderful vocabulary for strange phrases.

Throughout all the talk Fred said hardly a word but it was easy to see he did not approve of the conversation. It must have recalled him the incidents and sights he wished to forget. Afterwards he mentioned that he did not care for that kind of talk, it was bad enough to have to participate in the terrible business without talking and even joking of it afterwards. Dear fellow, how often must his tender feelings have been racked by the awful suffering he had witnessed.

To replenish the larder a visit was necessary to the canteen and so the rain having ceased we walked down to that useful institution. Among other things we obtained some biscuits and munching these we walked and chatted until dinner time. By that time the sun was peeping forth and we were able to take out our food in the open air again. Tinned rabbit was the chief item on the menu and more fruit followed. Perhaps Mother remembers sending Fred out a parcel containing these uncommon delicacies. If so it will interest her to know that this was the occasion upon which they were demolished and appreciated. Dinner finished, we went out to the Trench Mortar Battery. I riding a motorcycle and Fred sitting and bumping on the carrier. Despite the discomfort he seemed to appreciate the ride for he had recently done such hard marching. We found his old friends easily. What a welcome he had to be sure. Unfortunately the battery was to move in half an hour but in that time he managed to have a word with all whom he knew. From the Sergeant Major to the private, he was received with warm handshaking and kindly enquiries as to his well-being. The two Scots boys were there and right glad they were to see Fred – or "Uncle" as they affectionately called him. How they did talk of old times, at Merville and Neuve Chappelle. But all too soon for them the minutes sped by and presently they had to prepare to march, but not before Fred had spoken to his sergeant and arranged a transfer through as soon as possible. As we all know this transfer was never to be affected. Had it been, dear Fred would probably have still been with us. It was to have materialised after the next turn in the line but it was God's will that for our boy there should be no "next time".

After saying farewell to his old comrades we went into a neighbouring field and sat down for a final chat before I left him. As always we found much to say and the time for me to return came all too quickly. At about four o'clock I took him back to Sarques. On that occasion I spent about 30 hours with Fred, the longest period since we enlisted about three years before. For being granted this and other opportunities of seeing the dear fellow, I have thanked God with all my heart. To have someone from home more or less frequently, meant more than we know to Fred. He has admitted that a visit from me meant very much to him.

It was almost a week afterwards, August 4th, before I was able to go to Serques again and that was while I was carrying despatches. For that reason I was only able to be with Fred a short time. He told me that in a few days they expected to be moving up into the line. Really it was surprising the indifference which those fine fellows displayed at the news which meant death to many and terrible wounds and suffering to many more. On leaving Fred I promised to go and see him the next day. Accordingly on the Sunday preceding what was once for us August Bank Holiday. I again went to Serques. That was in the afternoon. On arriving there I was very disappointed to discover that the battalion had left the place that very morning for an unknown destination. Returning to the Corps Headquarters I made enquiries and discovered that this destination was a little place called Ouderdam, not far from Poperinghe. I happened to be off duty next morning so it was on August 6th Bank Holiday that I once again set out to trace dear Fred. After much searching I came across his regiment in a camp on the road between Ouderdam and Dickebusch. He was surprised to see me for they themselves had only arrived an hour before. They had marched from a place called Steenroods that morning, a matter of 14 miles. He told me he felt in fine condition and his wound he could only feel occasionally. Strangely enough he said he felt more fit than before he was wounded and gave as a reason that he had lived almost on army food since returning to France, whereas before, he had always augmented the rations by private purchases. I recollect he said that the army food was quite good and ample and that I was never to believe fellows who said they could not get food when serving with the infantry. Leaving the camp we walked along the road and into a field where we seated ourselves on some bundles of hay. Needless to say we had some inevitable cake from home and munching this we sat there chatting. He referred to the fact that it was a general holiday in "Blighty" and that led us to talk about the fine holidays we should all spend together after the war. In that Belgian field we planned to purchase a motorcycle and sidecar and have a glorious tour through the homeland countryside. We talked of how we should be able to take dear old Dad for a ride whenever he wished it and how after working in stuffy offices we should run into the country during the summer evenings and thus refresh ourselves. Of these and other matters we talked until I was forced to leave him at about three o'clock. As I ride along on my motorcycle I often think of the plans we made that afternoon. Fred would have been delighted to have become a motorcyclist for he loved the countryside and the fresh air. How fine it would have been after the war to have toured the country with him. Fate ordained it otherwise.

As it happened the very next evening I had some dispatches to carry to a place not far from Ouderdam. Taking advantage of this I managed to ride over and spend nearly an hour with him and incidentally take him some books to read. Before leaving I promised to spend my next free day with him. Accordingly on the following Thursday, July 8th I set out early and at 11 o'clock I was again with Fred. He too was free for the day and so we settled down to have some enjoyable hours together. I learned that the Colonel was very reasonable and when they were at rest as at present, he let them rest. Except for a parade at 7.30 and an hour's daily physical exercise, they had all the time to themselves. He told me that directly the regiment went out of the line he had been promised his transfer to the Trench Mortar Battery. The billet in which his platoon lived was one of the well known Nissen Bow huts. It was quite comfortable but rather crowded. Fred and his three comrades occupied the right hand corner furthest from the door. The floor formed their beds and tables and chairs consisted of an old biscuit box and two petrol tins. I could not help noticing how tidy was Fred's little space and how neatly his kit was disposed compared with the others. And his bed place was free from mud which was almost unique in that hut. His nickname was again indicative of the respect he had earned – it was "Colonel". As usual in order to commemorate the occasion we decided to have a little feast. Unfortunately the little canteen could only supply us with tinned lobster and some Oxford marmalade. However, with these little purchases and some biscuits we returned to the hut. As it happened that day I had brought from our camp ample D. R's food stores, a loaf, a tin of milk and some margarine. For the first time since I saw him in France there was none of Mother's cake available – an eloquent testimony to the constant supply of goodies we both received from home. Nevertheless, with what we had there was the basis for a good "feed" – and really we made quite a good meal.

The desert of bread and margarine and Oxford marmalade caused Fred to refer to Fred Vowles for the latter was very fond of this particular brand of preserve. That led us to talk of our brother-in-law at Baghdad. We chatted over the times that were to be after the war, when gathered round the home fireside we should tell yarns to the dear old people. We referred longingly to those happy pre-war days when perhaps we neither realised what our home and simple pastimes meant to us. The dear fellow, however, said it was no use being impatient or discontented, it would soon be over and back again at home we should be. For him it was to be over all too soon, and he was to find eternal home of "peace which passeth all understanding".

Every incident and almost every word of the various meetings there at Ouderdam are indelibly printed in my memory. I recall that for army dinner that day there was a stew with boiled chestnuts in lieu of potatoes. How the boys did joke about these chestnuts. Fred and I had some and he spoke of how fond Ma was of these nuts we used to cook on Sunday afternoons.

It was while sitting there after dinner that the post came. Webster, one of Fred's friends, had a letter from his wife. In it she referred to the fact that she had seen Nelly Cearns who had mentioned her brother was in the same regiment as Webster. The letter then went on to enquire if he knew Fred. That was rather an interesting coincidence and on enquiry we discovered that Webster lived quite near home and his wife had been a member of St Mary's Church. The three of us then began to talk of Plaistow and the old haunts of our boyhood days and so we chatted on until tea time came round. After tea Fred and I set out for a walk towards the village of Dickebusch and as we walked we talked. Now as I look back on that evening and the few previous times I saw Fred, I realise that he was less gay and more thoughtful. His conversation was frequently of home, and he would speak with obvious longing of the enjoyable days he had at home a few weeks before. In short I believe he was thoroughly war-weary. The terrible sights he had seen, the awful suffering, must always have been a constant hurt to his tender nature which would never permit him to harm even a fly; and the hardship with the persistent danger of two and a half years fighting must have had its effect on even his iron nerves and constitution and cheery uncomplaining disposition.

It was during that memorable walk that he referred to his work at Wiggins & Rihll. For the first time I heard a little bitterness in his voice as he said that if he had stayed at home like many others seemed to have done he would perhaps have had Mr Barnet's post with the firm. The bitterness soon went from him as he went on to say perhaps he would still have it after the war. At least, he hoped so. That was always what helped to sustain him – hope. While on the topic of his work he gratefully referred to the treatment always accorded him by Mr Rihll and the other members of the firm. He recalled what a splendid evening he spent with the former in London when home on leave. After that he once more spoke of the kindness everybody there in England showed to him. Yes! He appreciated everything that was done for him. When the war was over he said he hoped to repay them all. He was too modest to realise that whatever was done for him was done because he was so loved by all who knew him.

Fred went on to tell me that there was a big credit due to him in his pay book and in case anything happened, would I see it was obtained. In addition he added that all his possessions were for Father should he never return. For fear of hurting my feelings he would not bluntly refer to his being killed but put it in that way. At the time I wondered why he should speak in such a manner for he had never done so before. It may have been that he realised that the infernos of destruction and death into which the battalion was soon to go was worse than anything that he had experienced; or perhaps there was another reason.

During the evening Fred enquired about my own work and particularly asked if it was dangerous. As if it were yesterday I can recollect him saying: "You must take care of yourself, lad". Naturally I replied with a similar caution, to which he answered that he would "do his best as he always did, to dodge 'em".

And so we chatted away the evening through. For about 10 hours I had been with him that day and it seemed hardly as many minutes. With the thoughts of what he was to endure I felt I could not leave him but of course I had to do so. At about 8.30 p.m. on that glorious evening I set out for my billet. Just as he always did, he stood watching me as I rode away. Just as I reached the bend in the road I would always turn round and he would wave a farewell to me. Then slowly he would walk back to the hut.

The next evening I was able to arrange to take a certain run which would take me near to Ouderdam and give me another opportunity of seeing Fred. I was with him from about eight o'clock until about 8.30 that evening, Friday, August 10th. They were destined to be the last moments I would spend with him on earth, and every incident is clear to me. When first I walked into the hut he was sitting finishing one of the books I had taken him. He was surprised and very pleased to see me once again, especially as he told me the battalion was going into the trenches that very night. With me, I had just taken a tin of sweets and this simple homely thing was the last present I ever gave him. And how like him it was when he shared the contents of that tin with his comrades. When first I saw him he seemed quite cheery but as the minutes passed by he began to get more thoughtful and to speak of serious topics. "If anything should happen to me," he said, "I know you will look after the old people". Then probably seeing I looked serious, he added: "But of course I shall pull through quite safely". Too soon it was necessary for me to go and bidding farewell to his three comrades Fred and I went for a final few words outside the hut. There in the road by that muddy camp pitched amid miserable surroundings we bade goodbye to each other for ever more here on earth. These were his last words to me: "Well, old man, I hope I get a 'Blighty' one just enough to get me home for duration". Poor dear fellow, his wish was fulfilled only too well in the sense that he is at home and rest for the duration and forever. Finally he said: "If anything should happen through this, my accounts are all square". All I could say in reply, for somehow I felt indescribably miserable, was: "Goodbye old man and the best of luck".

Now I often wonder if what did happen was "the best of luck" and considering the many other worse things that might have happened I begin to think that perhaps my wish was granted after all. As on a last farewell we clasped hands – and sometimes I almost fancy I can again feel that iron grip of his – I looked into his grey eyes and found them strangely pensive and sad, so we parted. Before reaching that turn in the road I looked round several times to see him standing watching me out of sight and waving his hand in farewell, and that is the last mental picture I have of my brother Fred, standing there quite alone, so steady and strong, yet so tender and kind. Before him he had the prospect of an awful inferno of fighting before Ypres, but he did not flinch. He never once referred to what he was to go through, unselfish to the last, his whole thoughts were for those at home and the anxiety they would suffer.

To me, now it is clear he had a premonition of what was to happen. The whole of his motions and behaviour both on leaving home and when I had been with him, tend to confirm this. He was quieter and more thoughtful and sad. Then again the manner in which he referred to the possibility of his being killed was quite unusual, in fact he had never done such a thing before. As he slowly walked back to his hut, as he lay that night on the hard floor boards, I wonder what his thoughts were. Believing as I do that he realised his approaching end I think that possibly his mind would recall the incidents of the bygone days at home, at school, and at work. Very few things would he find with which to reproach himself. Then I believe he would think of Mother and Father and what they would feel on hearing their boy was killed. Possibly he prayed that God might give them strength to bear the coming blow – who knows but what strength with which his dear parents did meet that blow was sent by God in answer to that prayer. Then probably, with a devout request to his maker to give him strength and courage to meet his fate, the dear boy fell asleep.

That evening as I rode back to my billet at Eaquelbeo, my mind was very full. At that time I had no thoughts but that Fred would come through this battle as free from harm as he always had done. But even so, who could leave such a brother, knowing the terrible danger he was about to face, without experiencing feelings of sadness.

The night of Sunday, August 19th I shall never forget. It was when I dreamed a dream which first caused me to fear for Fred's safety. This is what I dreamt. I ride my motorcycle up to the trenches to see Fred, but could not find him with the regiment. Dismounting I got into the trenches. There were piles of dead bodies. Among them I searched for my brother. Presently I found him as lying in a sleep. As in my dream so can I see him now, with that smile we know so well lighting up that dear pale face. I looked and found he had been shot through the head. Awaking from my dream I found that tears were on my cheeks. Try as I would I could not sleep again that night.

Next morning I felt impelled to tell my dream to my close comrades. That day I somehow felt very despondent. Again on Monday night my sleep was troubled by dreams of my soldier brother, so that next morning I decided to go and get news of him. Time will never wipe away the memory of that day's happenings. After a scanty breakfast I went to the Signal Office and discovering that the 56th Division had left the trenches, obtained their location. My informant enquired if I was unwell, so that perhaps my dreams affected me. What a terrible ride that was. All the time something was telling me I should hear the worst possible news. Hoping against hope I rode up to the company billet not far from Steinvoorde. Into the yard of that farm I walked longing intensely to see dear Fred's cheery face. But he was not to be seen. Almost with horror I approached some of his comrades. In their kindness they told me they believed Fred was missing, but they knew the truth. Presently there came the sergeant of the platoon and to me he gave the awful news. Half expecting it as I did, it was a terrible blow and I had to walk away. These rough, honest fellows respected my feelings and left me. Never shall I forget their sympathy as they afterwards told me details. They said they had been expecting me and dreaded giving me the news. I suppose they could see that we brothers were fond of each other for they added, when it occurred they thought of me and how I should feel the loss. Later on the sergeant gave me a full account of what occurred for he was with Fred at the end – Sergeant R. Woolford, No. 233216, 3rd Platoon, "A" Co., 3rd London Regiment.

On Friday evening August 10th the battalion left Ouderdam for the line. During Saturday and Sunday they rested near Ypres and continued their journey on the latter evening. The appointed location for Fred's platoon was in front of Westlock and on Monday morning they entered their allotted trenches. This they succeeded without a casualty, which I learned was a very unusual occurrence. The trench was only three feet deep and was dug just behind the summit of a slight rise. In the rear the ground dipped into a hollow. Being recently captured from the Germans, the earth all round was literally mown up by the fire of artillery. Such was the spot upon which our boy was to make the "Great Sacrifice".

As it happened it was his first duty to do Sentry or "Stag" as they term it in the front of the position. That was at 4.00 a.m. There was intermittent hostile shelling but he came though it unharmed and being relieved at once at about 5.00 a.m. he got down into the trench for a rest. It happened he was next to the sergeant. Almost at once he went to sleep. Owing to the shallowness of the trench it was necessary to crouch down in order to obtain complete cover. Fred was content to sit with his back against the side of the trench, his head resting on his arms which were on the opposite side. Thus the upper portions of his body were practically unprotected by the earthworks. Can you picture him as I have tried to depict him there, in that shallow muddy grave, scraped out of the shell torn soil of battle worn

Belgium. He slept peacefully after that hard fatigue of marching and the nerve strain of outpost duty. Thus he quietly rested for an hour. Then came the fatal shell at about 6.00 a.m. It struck the ground just in front of the position. For a moment the sergeant said he was half blinded and stunned by the flash and explosion. When he looked around he was to find that two other inmates of that section of the trench were wounded and dear Fred resting just as before, apparently unharmed and undisturbed. "Are you alright, Cearns?" he asked, and receiving no answer repeated the question. Still there was no reply. Thereupon he looked closer at Fred and was surprised and shocked to find a splinter of shell had penetrated the steel helmet and entered his brain. For a moment he could not believe the evidence of his own eyesight, for Fred lay just as though he was asleep. There was a peaceful look in his face and his lips were half parted in a smile. His eyes were fast closed in that last long sleep. There was not the slightest sign of pain or suffering to be seen in the dear lad's face. Quietly, at the dawn of the August day, he had gone to sleep. Death must have been instantaneous and painless. There was no blood or disfigurement, but just a clean wound in the head about the size of a pencil. How good was God to take our boy so quietly and painlessly away from the world, which for almost three years had been a world of suffering and hardship for him. He took Fred away from the inferno of this awful war, away from the possibility of terrible wounds. He took him away from the terrible battle which was soon to ensue when our fine fellows suffered heavily, thus sparing him from the awful sights of suffering that were always heartrending to our boy. Surely he must have seen how war-weary the dear fellow was and so took him to his eternal rest and "Peace, perfect peace". Let me quote from a letter that reached me later: "A beautiful and peaceful ending to a beautiful life, as he lived he passed away into the better world. Being war-weary, it seems selfish to wish the dear boy back to the terrible strife and hardships he had endured, always without a murmur". This I think is a wonderfully true and comforting sentiment. The more we ponder on the last sentence the more we realise we should not mourn his loss but be thankful for the manner and peace of his passing, therefore in all reverence let us say, "Lord, thy will be done".

His comrades told me the stretcher bearers buried him in a little hollow behind the trench, wrapping his dear body in the very ground sheet upon which we had so regularly slept. As far as the sergeant could indicate I obtained the position of the grave. For reference I had better quote here what is known as the map location of this spot. It is I 17. B 3-8. Further he gave me a sketch showing how to arrive at the place. This I shall always preserve. In the battalion I learned that Fred was the first casualty but that during the same day there were very heavy losses. All three of his comrades were wounded. One of these Worth, performed wonders with his machine gun, being wounded three times before he gave up his post. Webster, acting as runner, was badly wounded in the face. Of the third and last of his friends, I could learn no details beyond the fact that he was wounded. Having learned all that was possible I went to see the Lieutenant Quarter master in order to try to recover Fred's personal effects. At first he told me that Private Cearns was in hospital and for a moment I had a great hope until I realised I had just heard the news from his comrades who saw him lying dead. Presently, however, Fred's pack was found and I looked through it. There was only his overcoat and a sheet and some socks besides some washing material. As I bent over these articles in a muddy field I felt very near the dear fellow. Everything was folded so neatly and packed away so tidily it spoke to me of him. There was nothing I could take away. On enquiring I learnt that his personal belongings had been sent to the base for transmission home. Plead as I would the officer refused to let even his brother have these things.

As I was about to leave, letters from a brother and his mother addressed to dear Fred were handed to me. These had just arrived and I opened and read them. How pathetic it was to read those lines from Mother, asking if he was quite safe as there had been no news for a long time, and praying that no harm had come to him. And then in the other letter those little brotherly items of news which would never be read by him for whom they were intended. There, quite alone, it suddenly came to me what a blow the news would be at home. Then I realised mine was the duty to soften the blow as well as I could.

That afternoon, sitting quietly on a meadow, by a little street at the rear of my billet, I was given the strength and ability to write a letter conveying the dread tidings. I have thanked God for the strength he gave me to do this. As I wrote those lines I confess that tears were in my eyes to think of the loss those at home and even I had sustained. Then I felt that these were selfish feelings perhaps, that one soldier here was at rest and therefore we should not wish him back to the awful strife and suffering. Could he have been able to give us a message I am convinced he would have wished us not to mourn him, but to remember that his end was quiet and painless when it might have been so different, and to be thankful. Then came the memory of his last words: "My accounts are all square." This now had a double significance. He only referred to his monetary matters, but how equally the words could be applied to his accounts with his neighbours here on earth, by whom he was so respected and loved. There was no person against whom he had animosity or who bore him animosity. Thus he dies "all square" with the world. And in all reverence I feel I can say his heavenly accounts were equally "all square". When my time comes as it must to all of us I pray that I may be as fit to meet my maker as my dear brother Fred. Noble, unselfish, loving and loved and a true Christian. There on the battlefield in front of shattered Ypres he fell – giving his life for his country and us, in a shallow and perhaps unmarked grave he lies. Wherever that grave may be, if unknown and neglected, let us remember his soul is at rest in heaven. Let us recall the reason of his death, the Great Sacrifice and then let us honour his memory for ever and pray "May God rest his soul".

I should like to conclude these pages with a quotation from a speech by Mr Lloyd George.

"The anguish of hundreds of thousands of homes is too profound to be expressed in words; but, judging the multitude of them, I know not, by those whom I know, there is not one of them who would recall the valiant dead to life at the price of their country's honour. The example of these brave men who have fallen has reached the life and exalted the purpose of us all. For ages to come there will be stories to tell of chivalrous men who gave their young lives for justice, right and freedom."

Such are the sentiments of those eminent Statesmen and such too I believe are the sentiments of the father and mother and sisters and brothers of Frederick Earnest Cearns, hero, gentleman and Christian.

THE END

- : -: -: -:- : -: -: -:- : -: -: -:- : -: -: -:- : -: -: -:- : -: -: -:- : -: -: -:- : -: -: -:

- : -: -: -:

In Flanders Fields

—

In Flanders fields the poppies blow
Between the crosses, row on row,
That mark our place; and in the sky
The larks, still bravely singing, fly
Scarce heard amid the guns below.

We are the Dead. Short days ago
We lived, felt dawn, saw sunset glow,
Loved, and were loved, and now we lie
In Flanders fields.

Take up our quarrel with the foe:
To you from failing hands we throw
The torch; be yours to hold it high.
If ye break faith with us who die
We shall not sleep, though poppies grow
In Flanders fields

Punch
Dec 8 - 1915

John McCrae

We Shall Keep The faith

Oh! You who sleep in Flanders Fields,
Sleep sweet – to rise anew!
We caught the torch you threw
And holding high, we keep the faith
With all who died.

We cherish too, the poppy red
That grows on fields where valor led;
It seems to signal to the skies
That blood of heroes never dies,
But lends a lustre to the red
Of the flower that blooms above the dead
In Flanders Fields

And now the Torch and Poppy Red
We wear in honour of our dead
Fear not that ye have died for naught;
We'll teach the lesson that ye wrought
In Flanders Fields.

In Flanders Fields **(facing page) is one of the best known WW1 poems. Major John McCrae was a doctor in the Canadian Army and wrote it when working at a casualty centre by the front line near Ypres in May 1915.**

We Shall Keep The Faith **(above) was written in 1918 by an American Moina Michael after she had read McCrae's poem. She went on to conceive the idea of using poppies as a symbol of remembrance for those who served in World War 1.**

CERTIFIED COPY OF AN ENTRY OF BIRTH

GIVEN AT THE GENERAL REGISTER OFFICE

Application Number 2707036-1

REGISTRATION DISTRICT WEST HAM

1889 BIRTH in the Sub-district of West Ham in the County of Essex

Columns:-	1	2	3	4	5	6	7	8	9	10
No.	When and where born	Name, if any	Sex	Name and surname of father	Name, surname and maiden surname of mother	Occupation of father	Signature, description and residence of informant	When registered	Signature of registrar	Name entered after registration
219	Twenty sixth January 1889 72 Swanscomb Street Plaistow West Ham U.S.D.	Frederick Ernest	Boy	James William Youngs Cearns	Elizabeth Ann Cearns formerly Holmes	Mercantile Clerk	E. A. Cearns mother 72 Swanscomb Street Plaistow	Fifteenth March 1889	[illegible] Registrar	

CERTIFIED to be a true copy of an entry in the certified copy of a Register of Births in the District above mentioned.

Given at the GENERAL REGISTER OFFICE, under the Seal of the said Office, the 5th day of October 2010

BXCE 721825

GENERAL REGISTER OFFICE ✕ ENGLAND ✕

SBM

Fred's birth certificate shows that he was born in January 1889. The family were then living at the grocers shop in Swanscomb Street, Canning Town, which was run by his mother.

JWY (Jimmy) Cearns and his wife Elizabeth and their family in about 1896. There were 13 children born but two died in childhood, including Bertie, the subject of the carried picture. Seven-year-old Fred is front row on the left and in front of mother is Percy. Yes, boys were dressed like that then! Other brothers mentioned in the book were Will (WJC), who is second from left, and Frank, third from right.

The "Family Headquarters" at Plaistow Park Road as it is today. No.8 is on the left.

This photograph was supplied by www.essexchurches.info.

St. Mary's Church Plaistow where JWY(Jimmy) Cearns took his family for communion every Sunday. It was very close to their Plaistow Park Road home. Fred sung in the choir here, joined the Young Men's Club and later spent much time at the St. Mary's Men's Friendly Society. The church in the picture was built from 1894 to 1896, when there was a need for 1000 seats, but was demolished in 1977, as by then it was too large. The present, much smaller church was opened in 1981.

After all that involvement with St. Mary's Church, it was very appropriate that this commemoration was placed in the old church.

This photograph is reproduced with permission from www.newhamstory.com.

BATTALION DIARY: Extracts from 3rd London Diary covering 13th August 1917. Provided by Royal Regiment of Fusiliers (London) Museum, HM Tower of London.

1917

Place	Date	Hour		Remarks
Dicke-busch	Augt.7 to 10		First "D" Coy. 282 points Second "C" " 216 " Third "A" " 210 "	
(Contd)				
"	" 11		Battalion (less First line Transport) moved up to Chateau Segard Area H.30.b.2.0 1/20,000 Sheet 28 N.W. leaving Mic Mac Camp 1.30 p.m. Transport moved to Dickebusch Camp H.38.b.6.6. Heavy rain during afternoon.	
"	" 12 to 16		Battalion left Chateau Segard at 6 p.m. Aug. 12 to take over the line from the 75th Infantry Brigade. There were to be two Companies in front line and two Companies in support and we had to take over from altogether three Battalions. Owing to the nature of the ground and the darkness the relief was most difficult and was not complete until early morning 13/14th. At daybreak 14th enemy put down heavy barrage on our right front and rushed two points causing casualties. All day our lines were heavily shelled. At dusk on 14th we re-established our line on the right, prior to relief. On our right front enemy patrols were driven off with loss. On the night 14/15th	

1917

Place	Date	Hour		Remarks
Dicke-busch (Contd.)	Augt.12 to 16		we were relieved by 1st Lon-dons on left and 8th Middlesex on right, the Battalion re-turning to Half Way House to rest, except "A" Co. on left front, which was not re-lieved until night 15/16th.	
"	" 15		At dusk on 15th the Batta-lion massed for the attack,"B" Co. were to act as Moppers up for 8th Middlesex. "D" Co. were to act as moppers up for 1st Londons. "A" and "C" Coys. were in reserve to take post in our original front line as soon as the attack went forward.	
			The assembly for the attack was most difficult owing to the nature of the ground, the mixing up of units and darkness. At 4.45 a.m. the attack started and owing to the slowness of the barrage and the impetuosity of the men it appeared that all waves and moppers up joined in one thick line. For over an hour no reports came in, then both 8th Middlesex and 1st Londons heard that they were held up. The enemy barrage first started after the attack had gone	

Great nephew Martin Cearns near to the place where Fred fell and was buried. This is about two miles ESE from Ypres in Belgium and calculated using the army map reference recorded by Percy in the book. From this view in 2010 it is difficult to imagine how this scene looked in 1917 after three years of shelling and battles through horrendous mud, leaving a sea of water-filled shell holes and not a blade of grass.

This picture from the Imperial War Museum was taken in October 1917, just two months after Fred died. It shows Chateau Wood, which was half-a-mile from where Fred fell.

Name.	Corps.	Rank.	Regtl. No.
CEARNS Frederick	4/Lond R	Pte	3475 281228

Medal.	Roll.	Page.	Remarks.
VICTORY	TP4/101B2	170	K in A 13-8-17
BRITISH	do	do	
15 STAR	TP/16B	8	
Theatre of War first served in	3) Egypt		
Date of entry therein	24-8-15		

K. 1380.

This is Fred's British Army WW1 Medal Rolls Card. It shows that he earned the Victory Medal (albeit awarded posthumously), the British War Medal and the 1915 Star. The reference to Egypt covers his commitment to the Gallipoli campaign from 1915 to January 1916.

Name.	Corps.	Rank.	Regtl. No.
CEARNS Percy L	RE	Cpl	14260

Medal.	Roll.	Page.	Remarks.
VICTORY	RE/1/31 377	1630	
BRITISH	do	do	
STAR			
Theatre of War first served in			
Date of entry therein			

K. 1380.

Percy's Medal Roll tells us that he was a Corporal in the Royal Engineers.

And what happened to those that were left? Eldest brother James had by 1899 married Ellen Elizabeth Paynter who added another West Ham United connection as she was the sister of Charlie Paynter who for 50 years from 1900 was player, trainer and then from 1933 to 1950 manager. They continued the family tradition and had 12 children. One was named Frederick Percy. Author Percy, as he had prophesied in his writing, post-war had a motorbike with sidecar but alas not with the company of Fred. He also married and had three children. Brother Will by 1924 had joined his father on the Board of West Ham United and between 1946 and 1956 brother Frank was Secretary at the club.

Club photo for West Ham United FC for season 1924/25. Brother Will is second row from back, three from left, and to his right with beard is "Dad" – JWY (Jimmy) Cearns.

And club photo for season 1949/50 shows in the front row Will in centre, now as Chairman, and far left Frank, then Secretary. Second from right of front row is Leonard Cearns, son of Will, who had become a director in 1948, and next to him is manager Charlie Paynter.

Len Cearns was later joined on the Hammers' Board by his brothers Will F. Cearns (in 1959) and Brian (1962). Len was Chairman of the club from 1979 until 1990, when he was succeeded by his son, Martin, who in 1978 had become the fourth generation of the Cearns family to serve as a Director. Martin held the Chairmanship from 1990-92 and remained a director until the sale of the club in 2006.

The above helps to explain why West Ham United enjoyed a long-held tradition as the 'family club'.

A WW1 army dispatch rider pictured at Verquin, near Bethune in 1916. The motorcycle is a Triumph Model H, similar to that ridden by Percy near the front line. This photograph was supplied by *Armourer* magazine (www.armourer.co.uk), who published the image sent in to them by reader Raymond Shirley of Nuneaton, Warwickshire.